BEAT THE MACHINES

AN INVESTOR'S GUIDE TO WINNING IN TODAY'S FINANCIAL MARKETS

DAVID S. GOODBOY

Palm Beach Press

Beat The Machines by David S Goodboy

Published by Palm Beach Press P.O. Box 2911 Palm Beach Florida 33480

www.beatthemachines.com

© 2016 David S Goodboy

ISBN: 978-0692739594

This book is for educational purposes only. Decisions based on information contained herein are the sole responsibility of the reader. In exchange for utilizing the information herein, the reader agrees to indemnify and hold the author, Palm Beach Press, its officers, directors, employees, affiliates, agents, licensors and suppliers harmless against any and all claims, losses, liability, costs and expenses (including but not limited to attorneys' fees) arising from the use of the information, or from any decisions that the reader makes based on such information.

The author and publisher advise you to seek professional guidance prior to making any investment decision.

"In the end,
what haunts us
the most are the
opportunities we
never took. . ."

—marketsurfer

Table of Contents

About The Author

David S. Goodboy is managing director and founder of the **Palm Beach Hedge Fund Association** and Vice President of Marketing for **intrendX**, a Palm Beach and New York City based consulting and marketing company for hedge funds and private equity.

In addition to his role at **intrendX**, David has worked with **Adria Partners**—a Bond Lease Real Estate Fund, founded by world renowned philanthropist and real estate investors, Dr. Zell Kravinsky as well as, Dr. Barry Brian.

Previously, he learned the fund business from the ground up with the 5th Avenue, NYC based niche fund of funds, **Eagle's View Asset Management**, where he spent 5 years in concert with the CIO, who is arguably the top niche hedge fund investor in the world.

In this position, David successfully raised funds in the 8 figures and networked with many of the wealthiest and successful hedge fund managers in the business.

He has extensive hands on experience in the electronic trading arena, since 1990, having traded for a St.Thomas /Chicago based derivative arbitrage firm, with a hedge fund, and his own account.

David is well versed in technical analysis, tape reading, niche strategies, fundamental analysis and stock picking. His knowledge base runs deep and wide in currencies, equities, derivatives and index futures.

Mr. Goodboy held the position of stock editor/journalist at **Tradingmarkets.com**, an active web based financial educational company and content provider for Yahoo Finance.

In this role, he was published daily on the home page of **Yahoo Finance** and had his thoughts and market views distributed worldwide in a variety of languages. During his tenure at Tradingmarkets.com, David conducted a series of interviews with over 30 hedge fund managers, traders, economists, authors, academics and financial rouges.

This position was leveraged to gain access and introductions to many of the financial world's top talent resulting in a solid start into the hedge fund business. His views and articles are published widely across the web on a variety of blogs and sites under his own byline and as a ghost writer for several financial luminaries.

Earlier, David worked on the team that developed the world's first broker owned media outlet—**E*Trade On-Air** where he also served as a daily stock commentator, stock picker with **Jonathan Hoenig** and **Kate Bohner**, previously of CNBC, for a nationally syndicated radio program via Infinity Broadcasting.

As a note of interest, TipRanks.com lists David's stock picking skill in the top 6% of over 9000 tracked financial experts and in the top 4% of over 5000 stock market bloggers.

David resides on Palm Beach Island with his wife and daughter. In his spare time, he can be found fishing, kayaking and paddle boarding on the local waters.

My story

"Don't do it; the markets will wipe you out!" My Mother frantically exclaimed on the telephone when I stated I was trading stocks with my meager savings. She went on to say, "My friend's husband has financially destroyed trading T-Bill futures, stay far away from the markets, they are just too dangerous!"

Her words of warning only served to peak my interest in the markets. Heck, if her friend's husband was bankrupted by the futures market, imagine the gains made by the person on the other side of that trade!

My naivety at the time was truly breathtaking, but it was this naïve confidence that kept driving my passion through the early years.

Back when do it yourself investing was in its infancy; the problem was finding actionable information. We desperately clung to every utterance of a money manager in the Wall Street Journal or Investor's Business Daily. Not to mention following now what was obviously dubious sources.

Today, unlike when I started, we are overwhelmed by the financial information waterfall. It is exceedingly difficult for the new and even seasoned active investor to understand fully what is critical and what is merely noise. The purpose of this book is to cut through the deception and noise of the financial markets by providing the essential information needed to truly beat the machines.

Acknowledgements

This book would not be possible without the encouragement and support of the following individuals.

The love of my life and wife **Anna Pomeranets Ph.D.** Without your never ending patience, emotional support and ability to keep my feet on the ground, this book would never have happened.

My children, **Hunter, Haydn** and **Evanka Rose**, You all bring incredible pride and happiness to my life.

My risk adverse parents, **Stan & Sue**. You inadvertently planted the seeds of my passion for the financial markets by playing the Stock & Bond board game when I was a small child. Thank you for your love, guidance, and support all these years!

Dr. Stewart Lee, my first economic professor who encouraged and peaked my interest in free markets, finance, and derivatives.

Dr. Victor Niederhoffer who maintained an open door policy for me at his Connecticut compound and trading group. Observing the interactions between you and the trading team has proven invaluable for my education in the markets. Thank you for all the introductions to the world's leading financial minds and having the patience to teach me how markets really work. Victor is a true academic among traders, and trader among academics.

Larry Connors who first recognized my meager writing ability and provided a platform to obtain a global audience for my words and opinion.

Michael Covel, a best-selling author and friend, who encouraged me to put my idea down in book form.

James Altucher, a world class writer, market expert, and friend who showed me that self-publishing is ok and taught me the right way to do it.

My Evolution As A Trader

Change is not merely necessary for life—it is life
—Alvin Toffler

Being tired of living at home during school, I dropped out of law school and moved east to the suburbs of Philadelphia. Talk about a culture shock from my rural upbringing outside of Pittsburgh, Pennsylvania.

I chose an apartment complex on the banks of the Schuylkill River and went to work as a claims adjuster for Cigna. On the weekends, I would spend days exploring and fishing in the local waterways.

One fateful Saturday, I met a person who would change the course of my life.

Every weekend I would pack up my rod and reel and go to the river, stream, or ocean.

On one of these trips, I met a guy who was about my age. I noticed he was wearing very expensive Italian leather shoes.

I thought, "Why is this guy wearing these shoes while he is fishing?" I also noticed he was driving a new Jaguar, a car I wanted but could not afford on my salary as a claims adjuster.

I wondered how this guy was able to afford these things, so I started talking to him. He explained to me that he was a "trader." Not knowing what that was, I asked him some more questions, and he explained further that he traded the OEX index.

While in college, in the weeks leading up to and during the crash in 1987, he turned a $10,000 gift from his Grandmother into over $900,000. Needless to say, I was impressed!

I remember from economics class, my professor Dr. Stewart Lee, preaching negatively about options and what he called, "financial manipulators." Despite his attempt to discredit traders, the idea was firmly planted in my head.

My new found friend's success reignited my interest in the markets. We soon became fishing buddies and he slowly started to teach me about the financial markets and how to make money.

This was pre-internet and pre-real time quotes. There was a financial cable station at the time called the Financial News Network or FNN. My friend would studiously hand-chart from the ticker that ran along the bottom of the TV screen. He would also produce daily charts from the quote tables from the back of the Wall Street Journal. Talk about dedication!

He was a student of an old market player named W.D. Gann and leaned toward the very esoteric edge of market analysis. Therefore, in this very odd way, I got my start in active trading.

Over time, I saved a small amount of money, following his lead; we bought Kingdom of Denmark Warrants and promptly tripled the investment. It was unbelievable, and I was hooked!

My next trade was LA Gear, a hot athletic shoe company at the time. Once again, the trade was a huge success. I thought I could do no wrong.

He and I then formed a trading partnership named Risk Capital Strategists and raised some money. We traded stocks and options on the OEX.

We did well for a while. However, in 1991 we decided that we were going to take a position right before the onset of the Gulf War.

It was January 16th.

Both of us were totally convinced both technically and fundamentally that there was going to be a massive drop in the market, so we bought an enormous position in OEX puts the day before the U.S. started the military action. When Saddam Hussein launched the "weapons of mass destruction", the markets would surely panic and plunge lower. Make sense, right?

Needless to say, we were 100% wrong. The market just took off on January 17th, wiping out all of my gains and just about cleaning him out of all of his profits.

That is when I decided I have to reevaluate, and I started studying how markets worked, figuring out what I did wrong and why.

If all the technical indicators were saying sell, how could it possibly go up? Why did I lose everything?

This was when my true journey started.

It was 25 years ago, and it took me from the backwaters of technical analysis to the hedge fund canyons of Mid-Town Manhattan, and many places in between.

I have been fortunate to meet and dig into the minds of the greatest traders and money managers who have ever lived.

I have worked for an option arbitrage firm who had a literal money making machine and for one of the top niche hedge fund investors on the planet.

Time has been spent observing traders at a leading market making firm, and I have talked with/interviewed traders from all walks of life about their trials, tribulations, wins, and losses. It has been a humbling yet exceedingly educational experience.

This book details some of what I have learned on this journey. Understanding its content will enable you to beat the machines. Not at their own game, but at the only game that really matters. The game of earning consistent profits from the financial markets.

Let's get started!

Why Beat The Machines?

It can only be attributed to human error
—Hal 9000

You are no longer trading against human traders with all their foibles and weakness. Your new competitors are the algorithmic high-frequency trading machines. These emotionless robots have taken over the financial markets.

Earning consistent money in the financial markets has always been a challenging game for the individual investor. Today, thanks to the proliferation of computer driven trading machines, profiting has become exponentially more challenging.

The combination of high-frequency trading, by which 10000 trades take place per second, decimalization, and ultra-tight bid/ask spreads have removed nearly every profitable edge from the active financial trader.

During the time of the Small Order Execution System SOES, the individual trader had an advantage over the big money players and institutions. Now, the tables have turned, and the majority of active traders are having their accounts destroyed. The high-speed algorithmic trading programs know all the tricks and tactics of the active trader and use this knowledge to win one trade at a time. *If it seems like the market has been rigged against you, you are right!* The at home, active investor simply cannot compete with the speed, agility and pure ruthlessness of the algorithmic trading machines.

Over 70% of all market volume is driven by these automated programs. The fast money is no longer available for the average investor.

I will never forget my first exposure to the world of high frequency trading world. The fund manager I was working for in mid-town Manhattan said, "I want to show you something" and we entered a small room off the main corridor of the fund's offices. As a note of interest, noted financial guru, popular blogger and friend James A. leased a room just a few doors down.

As we were entering the room, several stern, Eastern European quants who were recently hired away from George Soros were leaving chatting in Russian. On the left side of the room were four monitors with what looked like bid and ask prices just scrolling by at an incredible rate of speed. I could not believe the speed of what I was witnessing. These were the trades taking place at fractions of a second each. Exploiting the spread, latency, and outdated regulations, this was the start of the new era in financial markets. The year was 2005 and nothing has ever been the same since.

Not only that, but also the common knowledge surrounding the financial markets is simply wrong. It is propagated by brokers and other who profit from your trading. Always remember, the markets are a jungle and you are the prey.

However, the individual can still profit handsomely by actively trading. It takes more knowledge about the markets than was ever required in the past. You need to know the how, why, and what of how markets work to consistently extract profits in the age of the trading machine.

I firmly believe that the individual trader can still consistently extract profits despite the machines. There are a number of reasons for this with the primary ones being:

1. The ability to hold trades

Most algorithmic trading machines are designed to hold shares for a very short time. This can be measured in the fractions of a second in the high frequency trading game. The trader's ability to hold trades far beyond the short term focused on by the machines provides a serious edge against the machines. Longer-term horizons allow the true value of a stock or other financial instrument to be fully realized. Traders who can identify value and ignore the short-term machine noise are at an advantage.

2. Creativity

Until the machines advance enough to be able to "think human," they will always be forced to follow a particular program. The individual trader's ability to think outside the box can be a major edge over the market.

3. The value of the macro-view

The machines are primarily price driven. The trader's skill at interpreting macroeconomic events and how they will affect the financial markets is something that the machines are a long way (if ever) from doing successfully. Looking beyond price at the true factors that drive price is a huge edge for the individual trader.

This book was written with the goal of providing you with the knowledge needed to beat the market machines at their own game. Let's get started.

Preface

Do You Have What It Takes To Beat The Machines?

Oz never gave anything to the Tin Man that he didn't already have
—America

You are a unique individual. Most everyone is satisfied having a regular job and doing what they are told. This lifestyle is simply not appealing to you.

Your aspirations are high. You crave the freedom from worry and the ability to do what you want when you want.

Many times your goals and dreams are called unreachable and even crazy by the workday masses.

However, I assure you that your dreams can and will come to your reality.

I have no question that you are different, aim higher, and have the will power to achieve your goals. You ask how I know this? Well, just the fact that you made the effort to purchase this book tells me you have what is required to make it as a trader.

Introduction

Anyone can read a book or attend classes on how to do something. Remember back in college or even high school; you learned a variety of subjects but just how much have you applied that knowledge to the real world? If you are anything like me, you do not use 99% of what you have learned in school.

You can even embed market knowledge deep inside your mind, but this is not the same as doing it. I know this sounds obvious and straight forward, but understanding and applying this basic fact is what differentiates truly successful traders from those who just dabble in the stock market.

Believe it or not, it is better just to do a few things correctly than to know everything about the stock market for the successful trader.

The world is full of financial market "knowledge junkies" who talk a great game and possess in-depth market knowledge. However, when it comes to actually making money in the market, they do not. Whether its paralyses by over analysis or the pure arrogance of believing they know more than the market itself, no one knows. However, the fact remains that being a "knowledge junkie" does not translate into being a successful active financial trader.

This fact was made abundantly clear during my tenure at the St. Thomas /Chicago based option arbitrage firm. Our top trader was an ex-elementary schoolteacher who knew nothing about the markets. She only followed the system exactly, had no bad habits or preconceived ideas. It was much harder for experienced traders to execute the system, simply due to deeply ingrained biases and habits.

This book sifts through all the nonsense and misunderstanding in the modern day financial markets to provide a succinct guide to exactly what you need to know to beat the machines.

Chapter 1

Controlling The Demons Of Fear & Greed

Fact is fear will F** you up**
—Devil Driver

We have all been there. You are in a trade and it is going your way.
It is the greatest feeling to see your profit and loss screen keep ticking higher as the money seems to flow magically into your account.

You start to count the money and think of the things you can buy with it and how it will help your long-term goals of financial freedom.

It feels like this money belongs to you and you deserve it due to all the work that went into the trade decision. If you have experienced this, you know exactly what I am saying. If not, just wait, it is an amazing feeling.

Soon your price target is hit, but instead of following the rules and taking profits, you decide just to hold for a little longer.

Everything looks perfect for the stock to keep going higher, so instead of making profits, you are going to hold the stock overnight since you feel confident that price will pop even higher at the open the next day. This situation is a demonstration of the demon named greed.

In this example, bad economic news rocked the European markets overnight, sending the stock market spiralling lower at the open.

While your analysis was correct, nothing negative happened to your stock, the weight of the overall market, pressured shares sharply lower at the open.

The sell-off resulted in your winning trade to turn negative as your worst-case stop loss was hit, closing the trade at a loss.

Every active stock market trader can relate to the above.

Whether it is holding onto a trade too long, putting on too large of a position, or simply gambling in the market, we can all remember when this happened.

This demon named greed is a destroyer of investment accounts and even traders. Getting the greed demon under control is the first step to beating the market machines. Remember, over 70% of all market volume is computer driven. These machines have no feelings, no greed, and no fear. They are like psychic vampires feeding on your emotions.

Greed is one of the two primary reasons most traders fail before they ever get started in the game.

Greed is that overwhelming urge to risk too much and not follow your rules. While this type of greed is an account killer, some greed is a must for success.

There is a fine line between embracing the greed demon and rejecting it entirely. It is this line one must walk with the devil to find success in the market.

Good Greed & Bad Greed

It is this differentiation of the types of greed that is a must to understand. This is not talked about much in the field of trading education. It is a crucial distinction that can mark the difference between success and failure.

The good greed is why you want to be a financial trader in the first place.

You have a strong desire to excel in the markets; you want to provide a better life for yourself and your family.

You want to have the time to enjoy life and those luxuries like sports cars, couture clothing, travel and to indulge your personal passions. This urge is the good greed. Embrace the good greed as it is the driving force behind becoming everything you are meant to be.

The way I embrace the good greed is to set goals.

I like to post a picture of what I want to earn as a trader near my trading station, whether that be a new sports car, a large bank account or to be utterly financially free from debt.

Looking at this goal helps to make it real and put the force of greed on my side. You can do the same thing!

Now, let's take a look at the dark side of greed. The real greed demon. The dark side of greed is what destroys trading accounts and even lives. I am not kidding! It is a very powerful force that needs to be controlled and harnessed if you are going to be successful as a trader. The dark side of greed is what the market machines love. They love it when the dark greed grabs a hold of the individual forcing bad decisions.

The best way that I have found to manage this evilgreed is to start small when learning how to be a trader.

Force yourself to trade within your limits by only funding your account with the minimum required for your strategy. This will help you stay in control whether you win or lose in your first plunges into the market.

Next, realize that trading is a process. No one trade or even series of trades will make or break you.

Every trade is independent of the last trade, and it takes losses to have winners.

Taking the emotion out the trade by understanding this concept is the true key to getting control of the bad greed.

The Fear Demon

The other side of the greed equation is fear.

Fear is what keeps you from entering a trade or even taking any risk at all.

You are afraid that you will lose your money, afraid that you are making a mistake and a whole host of other rational and irrational fears.

Believe it or not, the key to controlling fear is very similar to managing the wrong kind of greed.

First, start by trading small size or even on a simulator so that you can learn inside and out how to use your trading platform.

Many losses, which are the root of fear, are from making simple mistakes on the trading platform.

Mastering your trading platform is one way to eliminate the fear of making simple but account killing errors that lead to fear.

$INDU Dow Jones Industrial Average INDX
31-Dec-2014 O 17827.27 H 18103.45 L 17067.59 C 17823.07 V 7.6B Chg -5.17 (-0.03%)
$ INDU (Monthly) 17823, 07

Fear and greed as represented by price in the stock market.

The next thing to do is to understand deeply that trading is a process.

The realization that success or failure comes from a series of trades, not any one trade is key to controlling the fear demon.

Beginners often have a difficult time understanding that professional traders have many losses.

Real professional traders even experience multiple days or even weeks of losses or just breaking even at a time. If anything, these losses do not cause fear in the professional trader.

The losses are viewed as a needed step toward the winning streak that will happen if you follow your plan.

The only thing that matters is the size of your losses and wins. Fear can be controlled by keeping your losses smaller than your gains over an extended period. Once you master this, you have beaten both the fear and greed demon. This is the most important step in becoming a real winning trader.

Chapter 2

Failure

Why Are There So many failures In The Financial Markets?

The first thing that every aspiring trader needs to understand is that the markets are rigged against you. The market is designed to take your money.

This is how it survives. It is why Wall Street is so wealthy, yet many of the participants are broke. Markets are a jungle where only the clever, cunning, and intelligent survive.

The public always buys high and sells low. The masses do the opposite of what is needed to make consistent money in the financial markets.

Some estimates place the failure rate as high as 90%. This means that only 10% of active traders actually make money over the long term.

Believe it or not, successful traders love these statistics!

Think about it for a second. You see, trading is a zero-sum game. Well, truthfully, trading is a negative sum game due to commissions but for this purpose, we can think of it as a zero-sum game.

A zero-sum game means that no value is created. Every loss is someone else's gain.

Therefore, the 90% losers only serve to greatly enrich the 10% consistent winners. A large group of losing traders is only giving their money to the few who consistently win. This fact is why some traders can build wealth at an exponential rate.

We have identified the primary reasons that most traders fail.

Avoiding these failure traps is the first step to becoming a truly successful trader.

Here are five reasons most traders fail (and what to do about it)

1. Buying High and Selling Low

This is the number one reason that most traders fail over the long term. Buying high and selling low is the easiest thing to do in the stock market. This is the reason why it is the number one reason for failure in the financial markets. You see, it is natural to buy high and sell low. Let me explain.

When you observe a stock making new highs, it is very easy to be tricked into the illusion that price will continue to move higher.

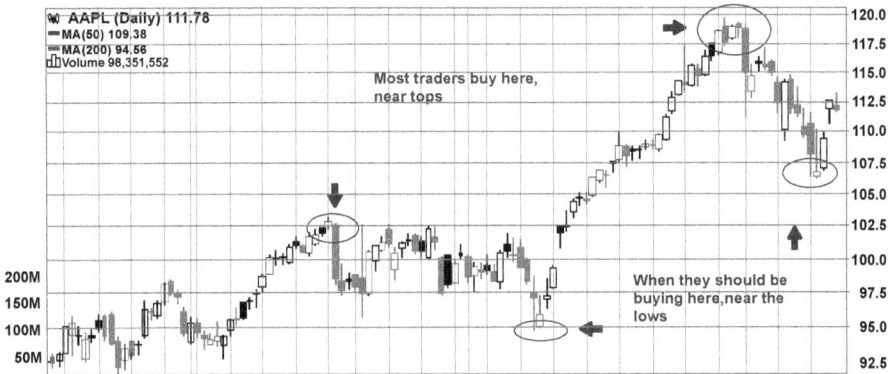

AAPL (Daily) 111.78
MA(50) 109.38
MA(200) 94.56
Volume 98,351,552

Most traders buy here, near tops

When they should be buying here, near the lows

—If It Feels Good, Don't Do It

It feels good to "go with the herd" and buy stocks as they are surging higher. However, it is precisely during these high volumes, upward surges that big money, professional traders sell their shares.

You see hedge funds; institutions and large professional traders need the heavy volume and substantial public volume to be able to sell their extensive stock holdings.

This is why sharp upward moves usually quickly fail. While this is not always the case and at certain times "breaks out" and "trend" trading can work, it takes much skill and experience to determine what new highs actually will last and what ones will not. In other words, the odds are against the trader who only buys new highs.

The opposite is also true. Most losing traders consistently sell new lows. After they buy the high, they hold on until their stop loss is hit thus end up selling at the lows.

—The Max Pain Theory

Often, losing traders do not even use stop losses but hold onto losing positions until the pain of holding becomes so great that they are forced to sell. This is called the "Max Pain" theory.

The "Max Pain" theory states that traders will hold onto losing positions until they are forced out. You see, psychologically, we are wired not to give up and believe in every decision we make.

This internal wiring spells the near certain death of losing traders as they continuously wait for Max Pain to close their losing positions.

Successful traders do the opposite. They love to buy stocks at a discount and wait for times of Max Pain for the majority of traders before starting to snap up the stock at a discount.

Simply stated, successful traders do the opposite of the majority of losing traders.

This means they buy cheap and sell high. Buying low and selling high places you on the same side as the big professional money and is one of the primary keys to success in the trading business.

2. Trade Too Large

Improper position sizing or trading too large is a primary way most traders lose in the stock market.

Greed is what causes traders to take on too big of a position. When a position that is too large relative to your account size goes against you, your account may be quickly wiped out. Risking too much on any single trade is a sure way to join the majority of losing traders.

You see, trading is a process not a single guess on the market. Consistently successful traders understand that no one single trade makes the difference between success and failure in the stock market.

In fact, the majority of a successful trader's trades may be losers. However, several big winners will earn the winning trader substantial profits despite the losses.

The leverage available in the stock market makes trading too large exceedingly easy. This is why many traders fall into this trap.

It is critical to remember that large is relative. This means that it is directly connected to your account size. If you have a million-dollar account, you can safely trade much larger size than someone with just a few thousand in their account.

The best way to look at it is regarding percentage risked on each trade. Some successful traders only risk 1% of their account size on any single trade idea. Others, I have known, risk up to 10% of their account size on a single trade. It depends on your skill in identifying high reward trading setups.

A good rule of thumb is to risk 3-5% per trade for the average trader. Any smaller and your winners will not have the impact needed, and any higher makes the risk simply too great.

3. Overtrading

Most want to be financial traders cannot wait to start trading in the markets.

Visions of great wealth and success drive traders to jump into the market. Once many new traders start actually trading, they quickly jump from one instrument to the next.

Not only do they jump from one stock or instrument to the next, but they also take profits too quickly and let losers ride. Overtrading is a sure way to failure in the stock market.

The reason being is that commissions, even though they are at record lows, quickly eat away at an over trader's account.

Win or lose, commissions and trading fees must be paid with every transaction. These costs may seem small, but they add up to truly counteract any profits that may be earned by those who over trade.

The key to avoiding overtrading is to use patience and to have a plan. The market will always be here; there is no reason to try to force a trade just for the action.

Gamblers try to force trades for the action, not successful traders. The machines and the market itself thrive on you over trading. That is why there is so much encouragement for rapid fire trading in the financial world.

Using patience to wait for the right set up is the smart way to avoid overtrading. If you catch yourself trading just for the sake of trading, stop!

4. Not having or following a plan

Having a trading plan is one way to identify a successful trader. Now, I am not talking about some mishmash mental plan that can change all the time.

When I say the plan, I mean a written plan that you religiously follow in your trading.

The plan needs to be drafted to prevent changing it to fit your mood or situation at the time. The power of a plan is to force you to do the right thing no matter how difficult at the time.

The plan needs to consist of what you consider being smart trading set ups, how many times a day or week you want to trade, how much you want to risk with each trade when to take profits and a host of other trading rules.

I find it best to distil my plan into easy to read snippets then actually post this paper next to my trading screens. It serves as a constant reminder just how critical following the plan is for the winning trader.

5. Searching for the secret

This may come as a surprise for some of you, but there is NO SECRET to trading success. Traders are bombarded with marketing and other advertisements that purport to provide the secret to success in trading. While some of this information can be quality and provide a few tricks or techniques, secrets just do not exist in the stock market.

Many traders have wasted countless dollars and years of effort trying to locate the secret to stock market success. This time, would have been much better spent learning how the stock market works.

Selling these supposed secrets is another way the market takes to want to be successful trader's money.

However, if I was forced to list the one secret to long-term trading success, I would have to say, self-control.

Controlling your emotions is a secret that cannot be bought at any price. If you insist on learning the secret, practice controlling your fear and greed as this is the key to success. It is not a secret, just tough for most people at the start.

Chapter 3

The Mechanics

It is in your moments of decision that your destiny is shaped
—Tony Robbins

The Entry is 85% of the Trade!

There is a hot debate in trading circles. In fact, it can be safely said that this topic is one of the top most disputed themes in trading the stock market. The debate is over whether or not the entry or the exit is the most important part of a stock market trade.

The traders who take the exit side as being the most important side of every buy and sell decision have an adamant argument. Their primary thesis is that until the trade is exited, profits and losses are just paper gains or losses. This means that no real money has been made, or loss until the trade is closed. While this certainly is true, profits cannot exist without smart entries.

You can be an expert at exiting trades, but if every entry is a loser, each exit will also result in a losing trade. Make no mistake; an expert at exiting stock market trades will certainly cut their losses short. However, without proper entries, they will simply have multiple losses and no wins. In other words, they will suffer a death from one thousand cuts rather than from one crushing blow.

Exiting is a paramount part of the trade. However, without a strong entry, the best exits will lose money. It is just a matter of degrees, but losses are still losses, which are unavoidable without a winning entry.

I will confidently assert that entries are 85% of every trade!

I know that I will take some heat for making this statement from the guys who are convinced that exits are the majority key to successful financial market trading.

However, that is what I have learned over all my years of trading. This type of disagreement is what makes a market. If everyone thought just one way, the market could not exist since there would be no one to take the other side of every trade.

Let's take a closer look at trade entries.

Many traders do not know how to correctly enter stock market trades.

There are right ways and wrong ways to enter trades in the stock market.

Knowing the ground rules for the opening of trades is a key to success in the market

Chapter 4

Five Primary Rules For Entering Trades

You have indecision and indecision is my enemy
—Afghan Whigs

Entry Rule #1: Use Limit Orders

There are two primary methods of entering trades. These methods are market orders and limit orders.

Most inexperienced traders use market orders to enter stock market trades rather than limit orders.

1. Market orders

This type of order is executed at whatever price the instrument happens to be trading at when the order is placed. While market orders have their place in fast moving markets, when used by experienced traders, nine times out of ten limit orders are the best way to enter trades in the financial markets. The market machines love market orders. They can do what they want with them. Avoid in most every case!

2. Limit Orders

A limit order pre-sets the price that you will enter the trade. There are different variations of limit orders, but they all help you control the price that your order is filled. Limit orders provide a measure of control in the uncontrollable stock market.

With limit orders, you know in advance what price you will get filled. This allows for proper planning for risk control and eliminates the chance of getting filled at a crazy price due to wild market action. Limit orders enable you to get a better price most of the time than market orders.

3. Preparation is the key

Planning trades before entering them is a key to being a successful trader. Most losing traders simply fly by the seat of their pants and enter trades on every whim while watching an ever-changing real time stock chart. This is a sure way to guarantee losses. Always remember that the market is designed to take your money. Without a plan, you will get sucked into every false move and trick of the market.

The winning trader plans every trade in advance. He knows just where to enter and exit each trade. Planning your actions in advance prevents crazy gambling type trades and assures that only the highest probability setups are taken.

4. Use Multiple Signals to Trigger Entries

Always make certain that more than one buying signal triggers before entering any trade. Make no mistake about it; technical analysis is deeply flawed. However, it is a tool that can help you be successful in the markets when properly understood and used. What I mean is never rely on a single trade signal. It should take a bullish or bearish combination of signals to support a trade entry.

Signals are best if they are technical and fundamentally based. In other words, if your technical signal fires make certain that there is a clear fundamental reason for the trade. It is the ideal situation. However, in the real world, knowing the underlying cause of every technical buy signal is not possible. In these cases, and this often happens, using several confirming technical buy signals is the key for higher probability trade entries.

5. Be Patient

Believe it or not, being patient is the hardest thing for many new financial traders. Practicing patience in waiting for only the highest probability entries is an original key to success as a trader. Sometimes it can take days before your set up occurs to enter the trade. Remember, sitting out of the market is just as important as entering the market. I know this may sound funny right now, but it is the truth for the successful trader.

In fact, being patient is so critical for success; the next section I dedicated to sitting still.

Chapter 5

The Art of Sitting Still

The idea of waiting for something makes it more exciting
—Andy Warhol

As a new trader, you are likely chomping at the bit to jump into the market.

You want to test your knowledge and build your skills to become a truly successful trader.

Believe it or not, this urge to jump into the market will be with you for the rest of your life. No matter how successful you become, the urge to trade never leaves.

However, this urge to always be trading can be very destructive. Trading is not something that can be dictated by the trader.

What I mean is that the market will tell you when to trade and when not to trade.

You cannot force trades successfully because you only want to trade at the time. Many traders try to do this by searching and searching the market for opportunities and taking trades that are questionable. This is a sure way to lose in the stock market. The truly successful trader patiently waits for the best trading setups entering a trade.

I have found that the best way to train yourself not to trade while sitting at your trading station is to realize that the market will always be here. By understanding that there is no rush to enter trades, it makes it easier to sit still. Also, this quote by the famous stock trader Jessie Livermore helps me keep the faith in the wisdom of sitting still:

> "It never was my thinking that made the big money for me. It always was my sitting. Got that? My sitting tight! It is no trick at all to be right on the market. You always find lots of early bulls in bull markets and early bears in bear markets. I've known many men who were right at exactly the right time, and began buying or selling stocks when prices were at the very level which should show the greatest profit. Moreover, their experience invariably matched mine--that is, they made no real money out of it. Men who can both be right and sit tight are uncommon."

Let's take a closer look at this famous quote from whom many call the greatest stock market trader who has ever lived.

Livermore goes so far as to say that sitting still is the most important factor in winning the stock market game.

Think about this for a minute!

He states that just because you are buying or selling stocks at exactly the right time, you can still lose money. The real key to making money is sitting still rather than buying or selling.

Remember, sitting still just doesn't mean not trading or being flat in your account. It means waiting for an entered position to work into profits or hit your stop loss. Unsuccessful traders often take profits way too early due to impatient. This is a sure account killer.

Also, new traders sometimes even move their stop losses when a stock is dropping. Sitting still and just letting your planned stop lose close the trade is always the best move overtime.

While moving stop losses and otherwise messing with your trading plan can work on occasion, over time it is a certain way to lose.

Truthfully, this is why it is so difficult to sit still. It is because deviating from your plan and trading works sometimes.

Make no mistake about it, the random nature of the stock market allows this actually to work at times.

However, it will not function over the long-term, and that is the key to success.

Understanding that winning as a trader is not about a single trade or even week. Success is all about executing your winning strategy flawlessly win or loss.

You see, overtime, a winning strategy will produce profits.

At the same time, this winning strategy will have losing trades and even losing series of trades.

Heck, I know an ultra-successful trader who has weeks of losing and just breaking even on trades yet has consistently winning years.

His trick is that he keeps his losses small and lets the winners run.

Stated simply, one win can make up for multiple losses when you are trading correctly.

The ability to sit still is a discipline that can only be learn over time for most of us.

It is certainly something that doesn't come naturally.

Learning this discipline can help in many areas of life, not just financially. You can "beat the machines" but it takes knowing what to know!

Chapter 6

The Argument

If it can be tested, it must be tested
—Victor Niederhoffer

There are two primary methods for making decisions in the stock market. The two approaches are fundamental and technical analysis. While both these analysis methods have their hard-core believers who firmly believe that their method is the only method, the truth is, aspects of both technical and fundamental analysis are needed to trade the stock market profitably.

Let's take a closer look at the technical vs fundamental argument so that you can understand how the proponents argue.

Technical analysts believe that all information is already inherent in the price of the stock. This means all fundamental data has been baked into the price of the stock. While this is true, the stock price is the result of all fundamental data, remember the stock price is the past, it has already happened. Technical analysts trade from charts, which by default only show the past. Therefore, technical analysts are buying based on previous price only. That is one negative aspect of technical analysis.

Also, there is extremely limited academic research that supports technical analysis as a viable trading method by itself. In fact, most rigorous and properly conducted studies reveal that technical analysis does not provide an edge when making decisions in the financial markets.

Unanswerable questions like, how many upmoves or series of moves in one direction increase the odds that the next step or series will be in the same direction, only serve to negate the value of technical analysis.

Is Technical Analysis A Waste Of Time?

Objective technical analysis without any other inputs is a sure way to the poor house for 99% of all traders today. At one time, objective technical analysis may have been used profitably. However, the machines high-frequency trading and a host of other structural changes have altered the stock market's landscape nullifying any edge objective, TA may have possessed in the past.

Remember, the high-frequency trading bots are often designed with the efficient market hypothesis as their core thesis. Therefore, when the majority of the volume is created by a theory that focuses on efficient markets, randomness becomes the markets defacto nature to an even greater degree than naturally occurs.

However, this is not to say that TA is completely useless in all cases. Technical analysis is a great descriptive tool. It is descriptive but not predictive.

I believe that technical analysis is best viewed as an untestable art form that can be useful since it provides context and a framework.

It is not an objective science due to the ever-changing nature of the markets. Some traders seem to have developed the ability to decipher charts intuitively and with the use of disciplined money, management creates consistent profits. Be extremely wary of any individual or service attempting to sell a technical analysis based program that provides buy/ sell signals.

At the same time, the anti-TA brigade would argue that it is the prudent use of money management that creates the profits. They say that the profits are made despite technical analysis and not because of it.

One of the most critical lessons in this chapter is that price is the result and not the cause of itself. Cause and effect is the main idea that technical analysts consistently get wrong. Price is the effect not the cause. Studying the effect (price) to project the next effect (price) is what technical analysis is at the core. This core belief is the fatal flaw of technical analysis.

Learning the factors that drive price, what I call Price Drivers, is a key to successfully navigating the financial markets. Price Drivers are a mixture of micro and macro factors that result in price movement. In other words, the cause of price, not price itself.

With this said, the fundamentalist crew only considers the fundamental factors in the stock price.

Without technical analysis, fundamentalists have no guidance or outline from a chart as to when to enter or exit a trade. Despite all the flaws of technical analysis, it does provide a framework from which to make decisions.

Sure, fundamentals can clarify whether or not a stock is showing strength compared to its peers and be an excellent judge of overall economic health.

However, when it comes down to placing trades, fundamentals are radically lacking.

The Solution:

Despite the failings of both technical and fundamental analysis, when used together, a powerful stock trading method emerges.

This successful method consists of using fundamental analysis to drill into the actual reasons a stock is moving. Once the cause of the price movement is understood, switch to technical analysis to time the trade. Doing so with the addition of disciplined money management is how successful traders make real money in the stock market.

Technical analysis is also useful for viewing the context of market as it relates to price. In other words, visualising different instruments or stocks compared to one another.

It is critical that financial market players understand both technical and fundamental analysis.

Chapter 7

What Is Fundamental Analysis?

If you get people asking the wrong questions, you don't have to
worry about the answers
—Hunter S. Thompson

Fundamental analysis is the study of the primary drivers that shape the future of the companies, sectors, and even the entire global economy. The goal of fundamental analysis is to make profitable projections about future price movements.

When dealing with individual companies, fundamental analysis involves the breakdown of financial information, a study of the management, business idea, and competition in the sector. This means looking at balance sheets, financial statements, digging into the background of management and the competition.

Using fundamental analysis in a broader sense with the entire sector usually focuses on a review of supply and demand for the products and services of the industry.

For example, if you are conducting fundamental analysis on the oil sector since you are considering trading Exxon Mobil, you will look at the supply and demand picture for oil.

The broadest form of fundamental analysis is the study of the national or even global economy.

This macro-form of fundamental analysis considers economic data to gauge the present and future growth of the economy. You may ask why this is an important use of fundamental analysis. Well, the truth is, we live in a globally connected economy. This means that the health of the global economy is often reflected in the success or failure of individual companies.

As a financial trader, it is critical to have a complete understanding of what you are trading. This means conducting top-down fundamental analysis starting with the global economy. I have discovered that this top-down method provides insights that are missed by the majority of traders.

Now I am sure you are asking just how to use fundamental analysis to project future stock prices. The way Fundamental analysis attempts to paint a picture of the future is to combine economic, industry, and company data to determine a stock's present fair value and predict future value.

If fair value is not equal to the current price, fundamental analysts trust that the stock is either over or undervalued, and the market price will eventually move towards fair value.

Fundamentalists do not believe in the random walk theory.

The Random Walk Theory popularized by the book **A Random Walk Down Wall Street** written in 1973 by Burton Malkiel.

This approach assumes that stocks take a random walk that is unpredictable for the most part. Adherents to the random walk theory think it is impossible to outperform the market without assuming additional risk. Most academic finance people are believers in the random walk theory. Most practitioners, traders, and investors, however, believe that stocks do exhibit price trends over time. Successful traders believe and can prove that it is possible to outperform the market by carefully selecting entry and exit points by understanding both technical and fundamental analysis.

The History of Fundamental Analysis

I have found that understanding where an investment method comes from can be a powerful way to grasp the complete knowledge of the technique. Believe it or not, fundamental analysis is a relatively new discipline compared to the traditional sciences.

A Columbia University finance professor named **Benjamin Graham** is credited with being the father of fundamental analysis. Professor Graham wrote two books that are considered to be bibles of fundamental analysis. These books are "**The Intelligent Investor**" and "**Security Analysis**." I strongly recommend that you purchase and read these books. It is amazing how the books grow with you. In other words, the more your knowledge and experience in the market expands the greater value you will find in these classic tomes.

Graham's students include the Oracle of Omaha Warren Buffett, Charles Munger, and William Ruane. It is indeed a great testament to the power of fundamental analysis that the greatest investor who ever lived, Warren Buffett, is an adherent to the method.

Chapter 8

Price Driver Analysis

A thumbnail sketch, a jeweler's stone, a mean idea to call my own
—R.E.M.

I created the term Price Drivers to describe my basic theory on analyzing the stock market. Price Drivers are the underlying forces that move price. Noticing the inconsistency and illogical approach of the pure price action/technical analysis adherents, I sought to define a method that focused on the cause of price movement rather than the result. Using the purely the past (price charts) to make trading decisions simply makes zero sense.

Price Driver analysis can become very data heavy when applied to indexes; however, it is quite basic when it comes to individual stocks. Although it can be much more quantitative, here are the basic building blocks of applying Price Driver analysis to individual equities.

Step 1. Global/National Economic Forecast

I know this may sound complicated to you, but it is easy and is the first step to conducting top-down Price Driver analysis for the individual trader.

The reason this step is critical is the global economy is what supports most businesses today. Understanding what is happening on a global scale is key to understanding the entire market down to individual stocks. When the economy is in growth stages, most industry groups and companies grow along with the economy. The opposite is also true, when the economy contracts or declines, most industries, sectors, and corporations drop in share value. Knowing whether or not the overall economy is expanding or contracting is the key to the first step of the top-down Price Driver analysis.

How do you know if the national and global economy is expanding or contracting?

The way I do it is first glance at China, the euro zone, and the United States.

Right now, the economy is expanding in China (although it has slowed down substantially), things are still growing in the United States since the 2009 bottom, and the euro zone remains the sketchy economy overall.

Keeping an eye on the performance of the major stock indexes in the three most important economic regions is the best way to gauge the expansion or contraction of the overall economy.

Here's a current example of how I start my analysis.

The United States via the S&P 500 shows expansion.

$SPX S&P 500 Large Cap Index INDX
2.Jan .2015 2:14pm   OP2058.90 Hi 2072.36 Lo2046.04 Last 2053.03 Chg .5.87 (o.29%)▼

$ SPX (Monthly) 2053.03

The U.S. has been in a
period of expansion
based on the the S&P 500

China via the KBV ETF that tracks a major Chinese index shows economic expansion.

KBA Krane Shares Bosers MSCL China A ETF AMEX
2-Jan-2015 2:19pm   Op 46.06 Hi 47.57 Lo 45.77 Last 47.26 Vol 65.4K Chg + 1.14 (+2.47%)

KBA (Weekly) 47.25

This ETF that tracks the
major Chinese inbox
indicates the world's
second largest economy
is expanding

Now, when you include the euro zone in with the rest of the world, the global economy is still expanding but could be showing a few signs of topping.

URTH iShares MSCL World Index Fund AMEX
2-Jan-2015pm 2:25pm Op 75.16 Hi 72 .16 Lo 71.13 Last 71.39 Vol 11.2k Chg .02.27 (-0.38%)

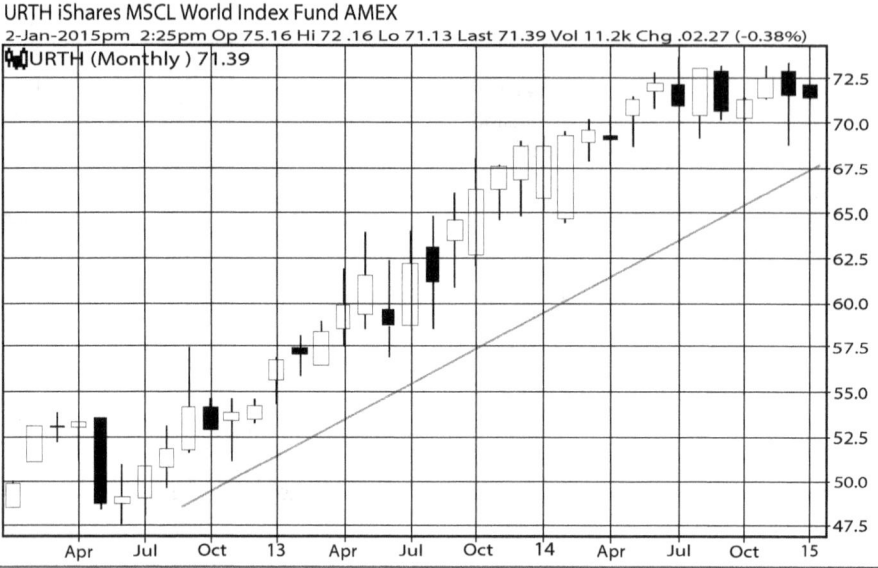

As you can see, overall the global economy is expanding. However, it may be signaling a leveling off or topping when looked at as a whole.

Interest rates primarily drive this expansion and contraction of the global economy. The adage that states when rates are low, stocks will grow remains true even on the global scale.

The above teaches how to quickly assess the world economic situation. Next, let's take a look at the next step.

Step 2: Sector Selection

Based on your opinion of the overall economy, you can make a wise decision about what sectors to invest in as a financial trader. Drilling into the right areas to look into is the next step of the top-down Price Driver analysis. An investor can shrink the field to those sectors that are most appropriate to benefit from the current and expected future economic situation.

Many times risk is correlated with expansion and contraction in the economy. In an expansive economic regime, the risk is considered low, and an aggressive growth strategy might be wise.

A growth strategy is one that includes purchasing higher risk growth shares like technology, biotech, semiconductor, and cyclical stocks.

If the economy is forecast to shrink, an investor would consider a conservative strategy and invest in stable income-oriented companies. A bullish defensive strategy is one that purchases consumer staples, utilities, and energy-related stocks.

Next, you want to determine the sector's growth potential.

This is done by studying the overall growth rate, market size, and significance to the economy. While the individual company remains most critical, its sector is likely to exert just as much, or more, sway on the stock price.

Remember, when stocks move, it is generally as a group. Believe it or not, it is more critical to be in the right sector than in the right stock! Locating stocks in a hot sector that are lagging the industry can be an excellent way to choose winning stock investments!

Step 3: Analyse the Company

This step is the final step to conducting the top-down Price Driver analysis. This step can be as complicated or as simple as you wish. The following graphic will outline the different aspects that analysts can consider when weighing potential investments.

Accounts Payable	Good Will
Accounts Receivable	Gross Profit Margin
Acid Ratio	Growth
Amortization	Industry
Assets - Current	Interest Cover
Assets - Fixed	International
Book Value	Investment

Brand	Liabilities - Current
Business Cycle	Liabilities - Long-term
Business Idea	Management
Business Model	Market Growth
Business Plan	Market Share
Capital Expenses	Net Profit Margin
Cash Flow	Pageview Growth
Cash on hand	Pageviews
Current Ratio	Patents
Customer Relationships	Price/Book Value
Days Payable	Price/Earnings
Days Receivable	PEG
Debt	Price/Sales
Debt Structure	Product
Debt: Equity Ratio	Product Placement
Depreciation	Regulations
Derivatives-Hedging	R & D
Discounted Cash Flow	Revenues
Dividend	Sector
Dividend Cover	Stock Options
Earnings	Strategy
EBITDA	Subscriber Growth
Economic Growth	Subscribers
Equity	Supplier Relationships
Equity Risk Premium	Taxes
Expenses	Trademarks
	Weighted Average Cost Capital

I completely understand that all these metrics can seem daunting for a new trader. Overtime, you will learn what parameters work best in the sectors that you are following. For right now, just being aware of these settings is a good step to grasping the final step in Price Driver analysis.

Putting it all together:

Fundamental analysis is the basis for two primary types of investing for the trader. These two types of investing are very different. However, in the words of super investor, Warren Buffett, these two types of investing are joined at the hip.

I am talking about growth and value investing. Growth and value are the two primary schools of thought when it comes to stock investing.

Let's take a closer look at both growth and value investing so that you can understand how they are alike and how they differ.

1. Growth Investing

Growth investors focus on companies that are expected to experience faster than average growth as measured by revenues, earnings, or cash flow. Growth investors also observe how the firm manages its business.

An example of this is the fact that growth companies prefer to invest in research and development, growth, and expansion rather than pay out dividends to shareholders.

While growth stocks provide the very real potential of outsized returns, they are a higher risk than value companies in general. Remember, we are talking generalities here and not absolutes. In the financial markets, there are exceptions to nearly every rule.

The truth is that growth stocks tend to do better than the overall market when stock prices in general when the stock market is moving higher. At the same time, growth shares underperform the market as stock prices drop. As a result, investing in growth stocks may require a slightly higher tolerance for risk, as well as a longer time horizon.

Here are three examples of popular growth stocks:

Apple (Nasdaq:AAPL)

AAPL Apple, Inc. Nasdaq GS
2-Jan-2015   Op 111.39 HI 111.44 Lo 107 .35Cl 109.33 Vol 53.2M Chg -1.05(.0 🖱 Hootlet
AAPL (Monthly) 109. 33

McKesson (NYSE:MCK)

MCKMckesson Corp. NYSE
2-Jan-2015   Op 209.06 HI 209.93 Lo 205.72 Cl 207.20 Vol 787.8K Chg -0.38
MCK (Monthly) 207.20

Autonation(NYSE:AN)

AN Autonation, Inc. **NYSE**
2-Jan-2015   Op 60.89 Hi 61.08   Lo 59.47   Cl 60.04 **Vol 901.6K Chg -0.37**
AN (Monthly) 60.04 04

2. Value Investing

Value investor's endeavor is to find proverbial diamonds in the rough; that is, companies whose stock prices that are trading for less than the intrinsic worth of the enterprise.

Value is a prime Price Driver. A truly undervalued stock will move higher over time. The trick is to know how to identify value.

The reasons for value stocks being undervalued by the stock market can be many.

Sometimes a company or industry have experienced hard times. Other times weak quarterly earnings or some external event can temporarily depress a company's stock price and create a longer-term buying opportunity.

The successful trader key to locating profitable value stocks is only to invest in shares with a margin of safety.

A margin of safety means that the market has discounted the stock more than it should have and the price at which it is trading, is lower than its intrinsic value.

Financial professionals define intrinsic value as the present value of the company's future cash flows.

Usually, value investors have a greater concern for the safety of the investment than the possible future growth of the investment.

This means that value investors often purchase mature companies that are often using their earnings to pay dividends. As a result, value stocks tend to create steadier income than growth stocks.

Here Are 3 Examples of Value Stocks at the Time of this Writing

Titan International (NYSE:TWI)

TWI Titan Intl,Inc.NYSE

Op 10.87 Hi 11.20 Lo 10.24 Cl 10.76 Vol 2.2M Chg 0.14 (-1.24%)▼

TWi (Weekly) 10,76

A M J J A S O N D 14 F M A M J J A S O N D

Western Union (NYSE:WU)

WU Western Union Co . NYSE
2-Jan-2015   OP 18.04 Hi 18.16 LO 17.74 Cl 17.93 Vol 5.5m Chg +0.02 (+0.11%)

WU (Monthly) 17.93

Mosaic (NYSE:MOS)

MOS Mosaic Co. NYSE
2-Jan-2015   Op 45.88 Hi 46.04 Lo 45.41 Cl 45.77 Vol 1.6M Chg

Mos (Monthly) 45.77

We have discovered seven keys for choosing value stocks.

Here Are 7 Keys For Picking Value Stocks

1. Rock-solid dividend yield.
2. Assets greater than liabilities.
3. Equity must be higher than debt.
4. The equity's trading price should be higher than the tangible book value.
5. PEG should be under one.
6. Ideally, the PE ratio should be in the lower 10% of all equities.
7. Minimum 7% annual earnings growth over the last decade.

Another way to look at growth vs value stocks:

Warren Buffett is well known for preaching the value investing mantra. However, many investors do not fully understand what this means. I like to think of value investing as a combination of dividend investing and growth investing but with a twist.

While the top-paying dividend stocks can be value stocks, as can growing equities; it is the way one goes about locating investments that add the twist to value stocks.

Value investing is a very popular stock picking strategy. It seeks to find stocks that are underpriced based on their intrinsic value. Value investors search for stocks that have strong fundamentals but whose price is indicating a bargain. The theory being that price will catch up to the actual value of the company providing the savvy value investor profits.

Growth stock investors look for stocks with soaring stock prices to reflect the growth pattern. Value investors take the opposite view searching for stocks that have had their share prices beat lower to the value zone.

It is critical to understand the difference between value and stock price. The two have very little to do with each other at times. Value is the intrinsic worth of the company. High-quality companies with long track records and favorite products/services have a high intrinsic value. Companies with high stock prices but weak fundamentals are not value companies. Many high-tech and internet type firms fall into this category.

One way to best understand value stock picking is to realize you are buying a business and not just the stock. The value investor sees him or herself as a company owner and not just a shareholder. It is through the lens of a business owner that a value investor chooses stocks. Value investors do not pay attention to daily fluctuations or market volatility.

Chapter 9

Profitability: A Key To Beating The Stock Market Machines

If all it took to beat the markets was a Ph.D. in mathematics, there'd be a hell of a lot of rich mathematicians
—Bill Dries

I am certain that many of you are wondering right now just how to use this information and what are the most important factors when it comes to Price Driver analysis. Well, it is easy, believe it or not. The key to stock based Price Driver analysis is to determine the financial strength of the company relative to its peers in the sector. Remember, our top-down analysis has already chosen the sector we want to trade, so now our goal is to locate the fundamentally strongest stock(s) in the sector to trade.

Boiled down, the primary determining factor of the strength of a company is called profitability. Profitability is a key element in understanding a company. Profitability is essentially, why the company exists and a key component in deciding whether to invest or to remain invested in a company. Profitability is measured in ratios.

Just what is a profitability ratio?

Profitability ratios are used to determine a company's inancial performance and its ability to increase its shareholder's value and to improve profits. Profitability ratios give investors the ability to look behind the curtain into the company's profits and how they relate to its size and assets.

Using this data, the investor can begin to createa hypothesis as to why profitability is improving or faltering over time.

Next, apply the theory to make an educated guess as to whether or not the company is overvalued or undervalued at the particular time.

One of the most powerful profitability ratios is **Return on Equity**.

The metric Return on Equity, or ROE, clarifies the profit earned by a company by deploying shareholders' equity. Don't be concerned! The Return on Equity ratio is easily derived and does not require any higher math to calculate.

Return on Equity is determined solely by dividing net income by average common shareholders' equity.

If you are wondering why an average is used in this case, it is because common outstanding shares can change greatly in number over the course of a year.

Companies buy back shares and float new share issues during a variety of times creating the need for an average to be utilized.

Just as a note, shareholder equity is defined as firms total assets minus its total liabilities.

Profitable traders believe that a business with a greater Return on Equity is a wiser investment than one with a lesser Return on Equity since the higher ROE means a greaterability to create cash; however, this is not correct in all cases.

Some businesses requiring fewer assets can have a very high ROE but still make a tremendous investment.

Deriving ROE (Dupont Formula)

PROFITABILITY X **ASSET TURNOVER** X **LEVERAGE**

$$\frac{\text{Net Income}}{\text{Sales}} \times \frac{\text{Sales}}{\text{Total Assets}} \times \frac{\text{Total Assets}}{\text{Average Shareholders Equity}}$$

ROE broke down into its simplest format:

Return on Equity (ROE)

$$\frac{\text{Net Income}}{\text{Average Common Shareholders' Equity}}$$

Chapter 10

Financial Health

We don't see things as they are. We see things as we are.
—Anais Nin

Now that we have briefly looked at the critical function of profitability, what are the other factors required to make an educated guess about the financial health of a company?

Remember, just because a company has one bullish metric, it is not enough to make a wise investment choice.

Knowing how to interpret the four primary financial statements is critical to success as an investor.

These four statements are the balance sheet; the income statements; the cash flow statement; and the shareholder's equity statement.

The following is a brief look at each one these critical reports.

1. Balance Sheet

As its name implies, a balance sheet balances the company's assets, liabilities, and shareholder equity.

Here's a closer look at how a balance sheet is created.

Assets and liabilities are the primary metrics of a balance sheet.

For our purposes, assets are everything a company owns that has value and liabilities are the debt.

It is important to note that liabilities can also include promises to provide goods and services to customers in the future

Shareholder's equity is the final item on a balance sheet. It is sometimes called capital or net worth. It is the cash that would be left over after all the assets are sold and the liabilities paid off in full. This money belongs to the shareholders of the company.

Shareholder's equity is the most important metric on the balance sheet for the active investor to understand.

Here's an example of a balance sheet from a major corporation. Remember, the numbers are listed in millions.

AT&T Inc.
Consolidated Balance Sheets
Dollars in millions except per share amounts

	December 31,	
	2005	2004
Assets		
Current Assets		
Cash and cash equivalents	$ 1,224	$ 760
Accounts receivable - net of allowances for uncollectibles of $1,176 and $1,001	9,351	6,901
Prepaid expenses	1,029	746
Deferred income taxes	2,011	566
Other current assets	1,039	989
Total current assets	14,654	9,962
Property, Plant and Equipment - Net	58,727	50,046

Goodwill	14,055	1,625
Intangible Assets - Net	8,503	429
Investments in Equity Affiliates	2,031	1,798
Investments in and Advances to Cingular Wireless	31,404	33,687
Other Assets	16,258	12,718
Total Assets	**$145,632**	**$110,265**

Liabilities and Stockholders' Equity

Current Liabilities

Debt maturing Within one year	$ 4,455	$ 5,734
Accounts payable and accrued liabilities	17,088	11,459
Accrued taxes	2,586	1,787
Dividends payable	1,289	1,065
Liabilities of discontinued operations	-	310
Total current liabilities	25,418	20,355
Long-Term Debt	26,115	21,231

Deferred Credits and Other Noncurrent Liabilities

Deferred income taxes	15,713	15,621
Postemployment benefit obligation	18,133	9,076
Unamortized investment tax credits	209	188
Other noncurrent liabilities	5,354	3,290
Total deferred credits and other noncurrent liabilities	39,409	28,175

Stockholders' Equity

Common shares	4,065	3,433
Capital in excess of par value	27,499	13,350
Retained earnings	29,106	28,806
Treasury shares (188,209,761 at December 31, 2005 and 132,212,645 at December 31, 2004, at cost)	(5,406)	(4,535)
Additional minimum pension liability adjustment	(218)	(190)
Accumulated other comprehensive income	(356)	(360)
Total stockholders' equity	54,690	40,504
Total Liabilities and Stockholders' Equity	**$145,632**	**$110,265**

As the name "balance sheet" suggests, the company's assets must balance with the liabilities. Here's the basic formula in an easy to grasp math.

The following formula summarizes what a balance sheet shows:

ASSETS = LIABILITIES + SHAREHOLDERS' EQUITY

A company's assets have to equal, or "balance," the sum of its liabilities and shareholders' equity.

It is critical to understand that dividends are a result of shareholder equity. Dividends are the primary way a company returns its excess cash to shareholders.

Always notice the relationship between shareholder equity and dividends. If the shareholder equity is in a declining trend, yet the dividends are remaining steady, this is a sure sign of possible trouble.

Also, it is significant to understand that the balance sheet is just a single picture of the company at the end of the reporting period. It is not a real-time tool that shows how the numbers were derived or the cash flowing in and out of the company.

2. Income Statement

These statements demonstrate the amount of revenue the company earned over a particular period.

The costs and expenses used to create the revenue are also included in the income statement.

The final line of the statement is where the company's actual earnings and losses over the period are listed.

Earnings per Share is the most important metric on the income statement. This metric reveals how much capital investors would receive if the company decided to distribute all of the net earnings for the period.

EPS is determined by dividing the total net income by the number of outstanding shares of the company.

Earnings Per Share (EPS)

Net Income - Preferred Stock Dividends

Weighted Average Common Stock Outstanding

The following is a sample of a corporate income statement that compares six years of corporate results. Ask yourself; is this a strong, financially healthy company?

Figures in million euros	2007	2008	2009	2009[1][2]	2010[2]	2011[2]
Summary Group Income statement						
Revenue	**2,578**	**2,505**	**2,461**	**2,348**	**2,594**	**2,707**
% change		(2.8%)	(1.7%)	n.a.	10.5%	4.4%
Cost of revenue	(670)	(627)	(592)	(601)	(653)	(678)
Personnel and related expenses	(583)	(598)	(606)	(588)	(640)	(681)
Depreciation and amortisation	(402)	(318)	(347)	(346)	(342)	(242)
Other operating expenses	(456)	(405)	(368)	(294)	(321)	(306)
Operating Income	**468**	**557**	**550**	**519**	**637**	**800**
% change		19.1%	(1.4%)	n.a.	22.8%	25.6%
Net financial expense	(286)	(375)	(177)	(176)	(219)	(169)
Other income / (expense)	37	54	(1)	(1)	2	55
Profit before income taxes	**218**	**237**	**372**	**342**	**421**	**686**
% change		8.4%	57.1%	n.a.	23.1%	63.1%
Income taxes	(26)	(60)	(102)	(93)	(122)	(219)
Profit after taxes	**192**	**177**	**270**	**249**	**299**	**468**
Share in profit / (losses) from associates and JVs	10	7	3	3	6	(2)
Profit from the year from continuing operations	**202**	**184**	**272**	**251**	**305**	**466**
% change		(8.9%)	47.9%	n.a.	21.2%	52.9%
Profit from discontinued operations	n.a.	n.a.	n.a.	17	79	277
Profit for the year	**202**	**184**	**272**	**269**	**384**	**742**
% change		(8.9%)	47.8%	n.a.	42.8%	93.4%
Other financial information						
EBITDA from continuing operations	**865**	**871**	**871**	**863**	**976**	**1,039**
EBITDA margin (%)	33.6%	34.8%	35.4%	36.8%	37.6%	38.4%
Adjusted profit for the year from continuing operations	**281**	**323**	**350**	**344**	**403**	**487**
%change		14.8%	8.3%	n.a.	17.4%	20.7%

3. Cash Flow Statements

Cash is the lifeblood of every company. Cash flow shows the movement of cash and if the company created cash.

Cash flow statements reveal variations over time instead of total dollar amounts at a snapshot in time. The information is obtained from the income statement and balance sheet.

Broken down to its core, the cash flow statement shows the net growth or reduction in cash during a particular period. Cash flow statements are broken down into three primary sections. Each division reviews the cash flow from one of three types of cash creating activities. These activities are operating, investing, and financing.

OPERATING ACTIVITIES

Cash received

Goods and services		**24,337**	25,925
Appropriations		**1,348,424**	1,294,468
Net GST received		**73,217**	70,105
Other cash received		**22,073**	25,668
Total cash received		**1,468,051**	1,416,166

Cash used

Employees		**527,752**	492,744
Suppliers		**775,223**	758,300
Borrowing costs		**4,299**	685
Cash transferred to the Official Public Account		**113,076**	119,865
Other cash used		**122**	44
Total cash used		**1,420,472**	1,371,638
Net cash flows from or (used by) operating activities	11	**47,579**	44,528

INVESTING ACTIVITIES

Cash received

Proceeds from sales of property, plant and equipment		**671**	57
Total cash received		**671**	57

Cash used

Purchase of property, plant and equipment		**33,577**	49,372
Purchase of intangibles		**116,392**	108,327
Total cash used		**149,969**	157,699
Net cash flows from or (used by) investing activities		**(149,298)**	(157,642)

FINANCING ACTIVITIES

Cash received

Appropriations - contributed equity		**116,227**	123,197
Total cash received		**116,227**	123,197

Cash used

Repayment of borrowings		**16,446**	15,166
Total cash used		**16,446**	15,166
Net cash flows from or (used by) financing activities		**99,781**	108,031
Net increase or (decrease) in cash held		**(1,938)**	(5,083)
Cash and cash equivalents at the beginning of the reporting period		**7,116**	12,199
Cash and cash equivalents at the end of the reporting period	5A	**5,178**	7,116

4. Statement of Shareholder Equity

This report reveals all equity accounts leading to the final equity balance including common stock, net income, paid in capital, and dividends.

Stated simply, the statement of stockholder's equity is a basic settlement of how the ending equity is calculated.

The question this statement answers is how did the equity balance on January 1 turn into the equity balance on December 31?

The way the statement is laid out is very simple. First, the starting equity is reported followed by any new investments from shareholders along with net income for the year.

Secondly, all dividends and net losses are subtracted from the equity balance revealing the ending equity balance for the accounting period.

Obviously, net income is needed to calculate the ending equity balance for the year. This is why the statement of changes in equity must be prepared after the income statement.

Here's an example of what a Statement of Shareholder Equity looks like:

XYZ Corporation
As at June 30, 2005
(In thousands of US dollars)

Current Assets		**Liability**	
Cash & cash equivalent...	5,000	Accounts Payable	25,000
Marketable securities.....	25,000	Accrues liability	10,000
Accounts receivable.......	40,000	Notes Payable	5,000
Notes receivable	25,000	Unearned Revenue	6,000
Inventory........................	45,000	Current portion of long-term debt........	1,500
Prepaid expenses	2,500	Current portion of capital lease obligation	600
Total Current Assets	**142,500**	**Total current liability**	**48,100**
Fixed Assets		Long-term debt	18,750
Investments....................	7,500	Deferred income tax liability	500
Machinery & Equipment....	60,000	Long-term capital lease obligations.....	7,500
Buildings & Land	200,000		
Intangible assets	75,000	Total long term Liabilities	26,750
Total Fixed assets	**342,500**		
		Shareholders' Equity	
		Preferred stock	20,000
Total Assets	485,000	Common stock	90,150
		Retained earnings	300,000
		Total Shareholders Equity	410,150
		Total Shareholders equity & liability	485,000

Chapter 11

Management Effectiveness: The Intangible Metric

After we analyse the four primary corporate statements, it's time to look at less quantifiable metrics that can have great sway on the company's bottom line. One of these more nebulous but bottom line influential metrics is management effectiveness.

Analysing this can be as simple as looking at the pedigree of the management running the company. Question whether each of the senior managers has experience in the industry, their education, reputation, and most importantly, what are they noted for? Today, just plugging their names into Google can return a wealth of information about the senior management. You will be surprised what you can discover. Be sure to weigh these findings against other stocks that you are considering in the same sector.

We have broken down this nebulous subject into four ways that the trader can use to get a feel for the ability of management to lead the company to profits.

The ability to interpret management effectiveness is one way to gain an edge over the machines.

1. Conference Calls

Listen to the quarterly conference calls. Many company websites have these calls archived so that you can listen in even if you miss the live version. Listen particularly to what the CEO and the other top officers have to say. Do they sound competent and knowledgeable about the industry and company?

The next most important thing to glean from conference calls is how the management answers questions. This can be extremely revealing of the truth. Listen to how the questions are answered. Are they answered directly and fully? Does the management skirt around the question without really providing an answer? Reading between the lines with what you hear is the key to get the truth from a conference call

2. Management Discussion and Analysis (MD&A)

This is an often overlooked section of the annual report. It is located at the start of the report. It is basically a management chat about their views on the company and outlook.

In and of itself, the MD&A may not clarify much regarding management effectiveness. However, the trick is to look at the last three MD&A and ask yourself if the management is consistent with what it says. Does it just repeat the same thing over and over again or do things progress? This is an ideal way to determine if what the management says meets the reality of what gets done in the company.

3. Ownership and Insider Sales

This can be the most telling of all the management metrics. The ideal situation for any company is to have the founder among the majority owners of the company. Examples of this could be seen in Apple with Steve Jobs and Microsoft with Bill Gates at various times during the company's past. This direct founder involvement at a high level assures that the energy and passion that was required to launch the company continues as the company matures.

What the next tell-tale sign about what management actually believes about their business is their ownership of shares.

There is nothing as bullish as management purchasing shares. People only buy shares in companies they believe will appreciate in value over time. Remember, management can invest their money anyway they see fit. Buying in their company, particularly large quantities are a very positive sign for the future of the enterprise. Not to mention, it can be tip off that something positive is about to happen.

However, at the same time, insider sales do not reveal much about the company. This is because people can sell stock for any number of reasons. There is no telling why someone needs to cash out of a position. Seeing sales is usually not a negative signal unless its multiple management at the same time is selling scores of shares.

Fortunately, insiders are required to report their transactions on the SEC form 4. The best free website that I have found that aggregates theinformation is www.insidertrading.org. Here's what it looks like:

InsiderTrading.org™

Insider Buying Screener: Stock Symbol

Begin Date: 2015-01-02   End Date: 2015-01-04

Select GO   Select

Buy/Sell	Transaction Date	Acceptance DateTime	Issuer Name	Issuer Trading Symbol	Reporting Owner Name	Reporting Owner Relationship	Transaction Shares	Price per Share	Total Value	Shares Owned Following Transaction	Form
Buy	2015-01-02	2015-01-02 21:38:08	UNITED THERAPEUTICS CORP	UTHR	MAHON PAUL A	officer	6,000	$33.1400	$198,840.0000	40,832	Form 4
Buy	2015-01-02	2015-01-02 21:34:21	UNITED THERAPEUTICS CORP	UTHR	DWEK RAYMOND	director	3,000	$31.1700	$93,510.0000	3,000	Form 4
Buy	2015-01-02	2015-01-02 21:30:40	UNITED THERAPEUTICS CORP	UTHR	CAUSEY CHRISTOPHER	director	3,000	$41.1400	$123,420.0000	3,733	Form 4
Buy	2015-01-02	2015-01-02 21:26:01	UNITED THERAPEUTICS CORP	UTHR	ROTHBLATT MARTINE A	director officer	5,547	$30.7500	$170,570.0000	5,687	Form 4
Buy	2015-01-02	2015-01-02 21:26:01	UNITED THERAPEUTICS CORP	UTHR	ROTHBLATT MARTINE A	director officer	4,115	$34.5600	$142,214.0000	4,255	Form 4
Buy	2014-12-31	2015-01-02 21:05:22	PHASE III MEDICAL INC/DE	PHSM	Prefi Robert A	officer	613	$3.2045	$1,964.3600	190,434	Form 4
Buy	2014-12-31	2015-01-02 21:05:03	PHASE III MEDICAL INC/DE	PHSM	VACZY CATHERINE M	officer	962	$3.2045	$3,082.7300	49,359	Form 4
Buy	2014-12-31	2015-01-02 21:04:44	PHASE III MEDICAL INC/DE	PHSM	Talamo Joseph	officer	710	$3.2045	$2,275.2000	8,339	Form 4
Buy	2014-12-31	2015-01-02 21:04:24	PHASE III MEDICAL INC/DE	PHSM	LOSORDO DOUGLAS W	officer	962	$3.2045	$3,082.7300	43,043	Form 4
Buy	2014-12-31	2015-01-02 21:04:02	PHASE III MEDICAL INC/DE	PHSM	Dickey Robert IV	officer	484	$3.2045	$1,550.9800	12,066	Form 4
Buy	2014-12-31	2015-01-02 21:03:44	PHASE III MEDICAL INC/DE	PHSM	Potter Stephen W	officer	921	$3.2045	$2,951.3400	14,016	Form 4
Buy	2014-12-31	2015-01-02 21:03:23	PHASE III MEDICAL INC/DE	PHSM	Pecora Andrew L	officer	934	$3.7500	$3,502.5000	346,078	Form 4
Buy	2014-12-31	2015-01-02 21:03:23	PHASE III MEDICAL INC/DE	PHSM	Pecora Andrew L	officer	2,018	$3.2045	$6,466.6800	348,096	Form 4
Buy	2014-12-31	2015-01-02 21:03:02	PHASE III MEDICAL INC/DE	PHSM	Smith Robin L	director officer	3,476	$3.2045	$11,138.8000	290,134	Form 4
Buy	2015-01-02	2015-01-02 20:17:35	PTC THERAPEUTICS, INC.	PTCT	Spiegel Robert J.	director	10,000	$51.0000	$510,000.0000	10,000	Form 4

4. Past Performance

Obviously, past performance is no guarantee of future performance. However, I am not talking about past share price performance. It is how the company's executives have performed at other companies that I mean. This is essential to knowing what to expect. Take a look at the lead executives past positions. Ask how these companies did and what the executives did to help the company. While this is utterly speculative, it does provide insight into what could be expected.

Chapter 12

Valuation: Putting This altogether

Now we understand the basics of Price Driver analysis and how to use it to make trading decisions. However, there is one more idea that you need to know to be a winning trader. This idea is what gives a reason to all this Price Driver knowledge. Not to mention, it provides actionable tools that will lead to fundamentally solid investing and trading decisions.

I am talking about valuation. The entire purpose of Price Driver analysis is to clarify whether or not a share's price is over or undervalued. Clearly, a stock that is obviously undervalued makes sense to purchase. While a stock that is overvalued could be a strong candidate to short.

The standard metrics that are use to value a company are the following:

1. Price-to-Earnings Ratio

This metric divides the stock's share price by its EPS or earnings per share. This number reveals what investors are willing to pay for each dollar of company earnings.

The lower the Price Earnings Ratio is the better. However, remember only to compare companies within the same industry. You see what can be expected in one industry can be considered very high in another industry.

$$\text{P/E Ratio} = \frac{\text{Price per Share}}{\text{Annual Earnings per Share}}$$

2. Price-to-Book Ratio

This ratio clarifies what investors are willing to pay for each dollar of company assets. In other words, what the company is intrinsically worth.

Here's the basic formula for the PB ratio:

$$\text{P/B Ratio} = \frac{\text{Price per Share}}{\text{Balance Sheet Price per Share}}$$

3. Debt-Equity

This ratio clarifies how a company finances its assets. This ratio can be important to tell how the company uses debt. A high relative ratio may indicate that the firm is using too much debt, which could be a negative sign. It is calculated by dividing all the liabilities by total stockholder equity.

$$\text{Debt - Equity Ratio} = \frac{\text{Total Liabilities}}{\text{Shareholer's Equity}}$$

4. Free Cash Flow

This metric reveals just how much cash a company is left with after any capital expenditure. While certain accounting methods can obscure these numbers, the free cash flow metric forces them into the open. Here is how it is derived:

Free Cash Flow
Initial Investment
+ OCF (new Project)
- OCF (existing project)
- change in NWC
+ salvage value
= Free Cash Flow

5. PEG Ratio

This is a version of the PE ration that includes growth in the calculation. It can be very useful in determining future growth. It is calculated like this:

PEG Ratio

$$\text{PEG Ratio} = \frac{\left(\dfrac{\text{Market Value per Share}}{\text{Earnings per Share}}\right)}{\text{Projected Annual Earnings Growth}}$$

Now that we have a full understanding of how successful traders utilize fundamental analysis to make profitable trading decisions, it is time to take a close look at Technical Analysis.

Chapter 13

Technical Analysis' Terrible Lie And What To Do About It

Most financial traders today get their start by using technical analysis. The widespread popularity of personal computers and inexpensive real-time data feeds has made technical analysis the default method that most traders use to make trading and investing decisions.

Things were not always like this. Before the personal computer, technical analysts had to chart pain stakingly by hand or use chart books that revealed long-term technical charts. It was an incredibly time-consuming task to use technical analysis correctly in the years before personal computers.

Today, the most technical analysis is automated with broker's trading platforms. Want to see the 200-period simple moving average on a one-minute chart, push a button, and there it is, want to compare the price action of several different stocks on the same chart? No problem, you can have that instantly. What use to take days or even weeks of struggling with graph paper is now done instantly, Let's take a closer look:

Technical analysis is commonly defined as the study of price charts to determine **trend** and **patterns**, that either is believed to repeat or signal something is about to happen. We will go in-depth into patterns and trend further on in this book.

Charles Dow is credited as being one of the fore-fathers of technical analysis. He created point and figure charting which plots price action in graphic form.

Dow is also famous for creating the investing thesis known as "Dow Theory." We will delve deeper into the idea further on, but suffice to say that most technical analysis theories can be traced back to the original Dow Theory.

The basic tenants of technical analysis were well entrenched by the early 20th century. By mid-century, additional pioneers of technical analysis such as Bill Jiler, Robert Edwards, John Magee, Alexander Wheelan and Abe Cohen were actively expanding the field.

The Terrible Lie of Technical Analysis:

Believe it or not, there are very valid arguments against the validity of technical analysis.

Like most new traders, I got my start in the markets via technical analysis. Technical analysis as defined by the study of past price movements and chart patterns. It all seemed to make perfect sense on the chart, however, when applied in real time, things did not appear as bright as the various TA proponents proclaim.

Buying breakouts above the 200-day simple moving average, selling touches of the upper Bollinger Band and the other easily understood TA tenants just failed to produce the profits promised by the gurus. Surely, I must be interpreting the data wrong, right? After many years of trading and market study, I have reached the conclusion that TA is simply a minor tool in the process toward success. Technical analysis must only be use as part of an overall trading plan that includes fundamental analysis and money management.

This is a critical distinction of the successful trader. Many traders get stuck in the trap of using only technical analysis to make decisions. This is a dangerous trap and desperate to escape from due to the basic psychological biases that make price charts so appealing.

Here are four reasons why objective technical analysis is a lie.

1. **Hindsight bias**. Charts are notorious for tricking the human brain into hindsight biases. It all looks very clear on a chart. However, what happens next has nothing to do with what has happened previously regarding price. Think about it. If you flip a coin ten times, and it comes up heads ten times in a row, have the odds increased that the 11th flip will be heads?

2. **Price is not the reflection of the herd**. A prime tenant of technical analysis is that price is the reflection of the crowd, the mass of investors, so to speak. This does not make any sense. Price is the reflection of the money movement at any one time into and out of the instrument. The capital mass can be controlled by one-person fund or several. The masses of investors do not control price any more than the crowd at a baseball game determine the victor. One hedge fund manager, who makes a decision on a whim, can completely change the direction of a security regardless of the herd's positioning. He who has the capital is who controls price.

3. **There is limited academic evidence of technical analysis working.**

    Aside from a few inconclusive papers by Andrew Lo of MIT, there is no indication of TA being sufficient enough to increase ones odds of a winning trade upon entry anymore than random chance.

4. **Cycles are always changing**

    Market cycles are constantly in a state of flux. Although patterns appear to repeat, there is no set pattern to the repetition. The past is not indicative of the future.

    Despite these major flaws, technical analysis remains a tool when it comes to being a successful trader. Technical analysis provides an outline or picture of price. This image allows pinpoint entries and exits based on technical reasons. Are these entries and exits always ideal? No way! However, using technical analysis as tool to time exits and entries can make sense as long as you realize its limitations. Remember, technical analysis' only reality is subjective to your own situation.

The simplistic, subjective nature of technical analysis provides a personal outline for action despite lacking an objective truth or accuracy.

Let's take a closer look at the primary ideas behind technical analysis.

Trend

Price trend is the core idea behind all technical analysis. Technical analysis teaches that share prices moves in trends. This means that if the price is moving higher, it is more likely to continue moving higher unless acted upon by an outside force. At the same time, if the price is moving lower, it is more liable to continue to move lower until something happens to reverse the direction.

Trend traders think of this phenomenon as Newton's First Law of Physics. Obviously, price has nothing to do with a physical object, but the idea still serves as a simple way to visualize trend.

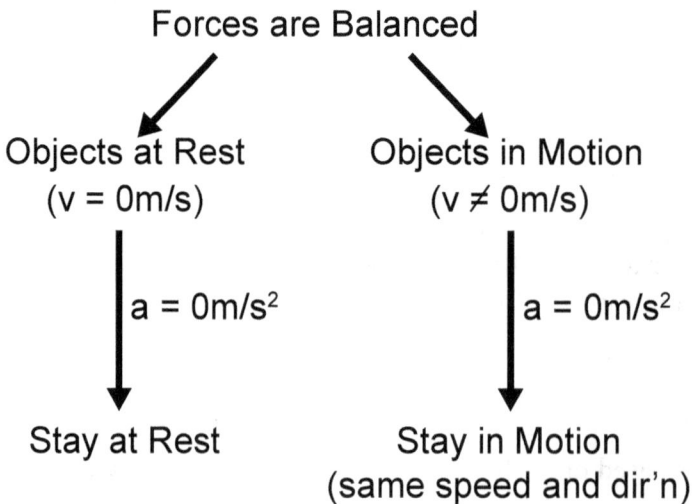

Forces are Balanced

Objects at Rest
$(v = 0m/s)$

$a = 0m/s^2$

Stay at Rest

Objects in Motion
$(v \neq 0m/s)$

$a = 0m/s^2$

Stay in Motion
(same speed and dir'n)

An uptrend is defined as a series of higher highs and higher lows in price.

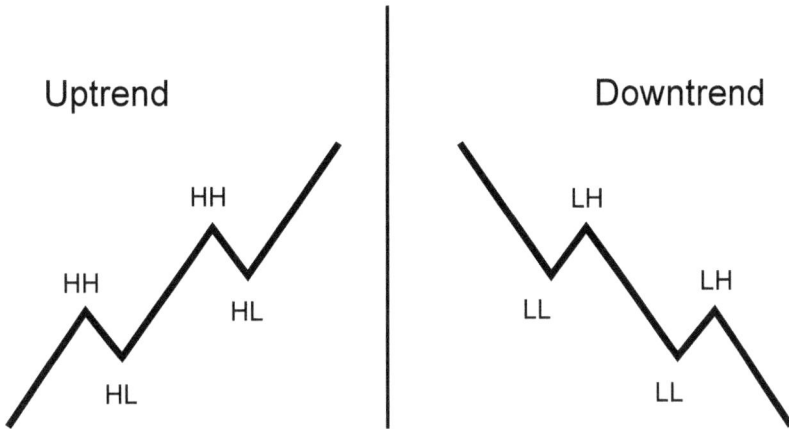

Uptrend

HH

HH

HL

HL

Downtrend

LH

LH

LL

LL

While a downtrend is a series of lower lows and lower highs, it is much easier to visualize than understand from words alone.

The goal of technical analysis is to determine the direction and strength of the trend. Once this is verified, the trader can make an educated decision as to what direction to enter the stock.

Some successful traders are trend traders. This means that they try to trade in the direction of the trend believing that the trend will continue long enough to create profits.

Other traders are counter-trend or contrarian traders. Counter-trend traders go against the trend expecting it to end and reverse soon. The best traders keep an open mind and feel comfortable trading with the trend or against the trend depending on what the market is indicating at the time.

This ability to remain flexible and listen to the market is an easy concept to grasp. However, in action, it is tough to execute. This is one of the most challenging aspects on how to execute trades in a trend.

Clearly, once you enter a trade, you would like the trend to continue in your direction until profits are earned. This is the key to directional trading strategies.

I have personally had many good spirited arguments with the high priest of trend following, Michael Covel. Michael has written several excellent books, in which one I am name checked, on the history and strategy of trend following. Although I disagree with him on most points, the fact remains that many of the most successful funds on earth have been trend following funds.

While I argue that these ultra-successful funds are merely the winners evidenced by survivorship bias, and that trend following is the only way to manage mega amounts of capital, Covel puts forth a compelling argument as to the veracity of trend following.

My experience has taught that trend only matters after you enter the trade. Before going into the trade, trend direction is meaningless when it comes to predicting the next move or series of moves. However, once the trade is opened, the trend becomes the most critical thing.

Think about it this way, if you flip a coin, and it comes up heads ten times in a row, are you in a "heads" trend?

Also, the public are trend followers by default. This means that the public is always buying new highs and selling new lows. We all know what happens to most of the public!

With this said, it is still important to have a basic grasp of trend and how the technical analysts determine whether it will continue or reverse.

Trend Following

Traditional trend following teaches that buying new highs and selling new lows is the ideal way to enter the market. Other trend followers try to vary the conventional methods by going long on pullbacks during smaller time frames within the overall uptrend in just like technical analysts, trend followers discard fundamental data thinking that price is the only thing that matters when making trading decisions.

How to Trend Follow:

Step 1: Determine trend—

Step 2: Ask what way is the stock moving. Using Simple Moving Averages like the 200 day is ideal for clarifying trend. Take a look at the daily chart, is it trending up or down? Let's assume your chosen stock is trending up.

Step 3: Determine your entry point— the best way to enter a trend trade is hotly debated. As stated earlier, traditional trend traders will buy whenever a new high is reached. Others will wait for a pull back to the Moving average, or a pull back within a shorter time frame chart.

Step 4. Patiently wait—for the trend to continue carrying your position into profits. This is the hardest part for most traders. Trend Following is a slow, grinding trading process.

Step 5. Exit the trade—Wait until the trend appears to have changed totally prior to exiting. This is another nebulous trend following rule. The question if this is just a draw down or an actual change in trend is a difficult one to answer in real time. However, it looks like an easy one in hindsight. One needs to follow strict rules concerning exits when Trend Following. Discipline is critical for this strategy.

The Problem With Trend Following

Trend following's primary issue is the problem with hindsight analysis and survivorship bias. Trend following proponent's points toward the fact that the largest funds on earth are often trend following funds. While this is accurate, the fact is that monster funds are simply not agile enough to be anything but trend following. In other words, buy and hold but spread the risk across the global markets. Using this method without billions in capital for proper diversification is little more than purchasing and hoping.

Survivorship bias means that profitable trend followers are simply the lucky ones. You never hear about the failed trend followers, just the ones who succeed.

Hindsight analysis means that it is easy to see trends on past price charts. It is simply to trick your mind into the would a, could a, should a trap of seeing huge profits by buying into trends. Unfortunately, trades are entered in real time, and it is unknown whether or not the trend will continue before the trade is entered.

Trend following is not quantitative. It is impossible to answer the question of how many upward (or downward) moves or series of moves increase the odds that the next step or series will be in the same (or opposite) direction; looms large against trend following. Not to mention the oft-cited comparison of a coin toss. If a coin is flipped10 times and it comes up heads 10 times, is this a heads trend?

Price Patterns:

The primary way the technical trader decides if a price trend will carry on in the same direction or reverse is by chart patterns. This next section will review and explain both trend continuation chart patterns and trend reversal chart patterns.

Before we start on the graph pattern explanation, there's a very critical point that needs to be made. **The point is that technical analysts believe that the stock market is fractal across time frames.**

What I mean by this is a minute chart will reveal the same price patterns as any other time frame chart. A daily chart will have the same patterns as a minute chart or as a monthly chart. In fact, without knowing the time frame represented on the chart, it is hard to determine the time frame in many cases.

This means that what you learn about price chart patterns can be applied to any time frame. In fact, some traders specialize in top-down analysis of charts. What this means is they scan for bullish charts on the weekly time frame, then drill down into the daily, and the intraday time frames looking for short-term bullish trades. Naturally, bearish trades can be located this way also.

Understanding the fractal nature of price charts is a critical distinction for traders. The examples that I will be providing you on chart patterns are all based on the daily chart. However, the same models are applicable regardless of time frame.

Remember, I am providing these basic patterns as being descriptive only. They are not predictive and their value lays in their ability to place the market in context.

Continuation Price Patterns

This section will focus on continuation price patterns. Continuation price patterns are believed to signal that the trend will continue in the same direction.

1. **Ascending Triangle**

An ascending triangle is a bullish chart formation that can be found during an upward trend. An ascending triangle is thought to indicate accumulation of shares.

Here is an example of an Ascending Triangle.

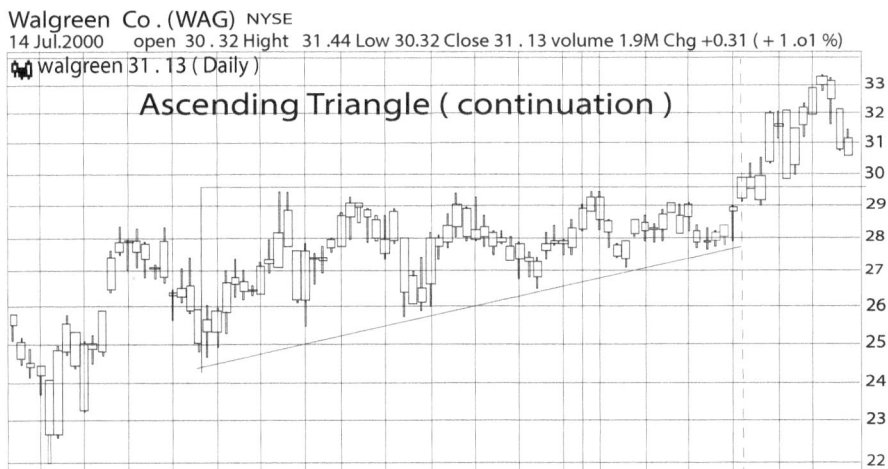

Walgreen Co . (WAG) NYSE
14 Jul.2000   open 30 . 32 Hight 31 .44 Low 30.32 Close 31 . 13 volume 1.9M Chg +0.31 (+ 1 .o1 %)
walgreen 31 . 13 (Daily)
Ascending Triangle (continuation)

2. **Flag and Pennant**

Flags and pennants are trend continuation patterns that occur after a sharp directional move in the stock.

Let's take a look at both a flag and a pennant continuation pattern:

A Pennant formation

Dell Inc. (DELL) Nasdaq Nat. Mkt.
19-May-1998   open 24.36 High 24.50 Low 23.38 Close 23.65 Volume 114.3M Ch

Dell 23.65 (Daily)

Pennant (Continuation)

This is a flag pattern

Hewlett-Packard Co (HPQ) NYSE
30-Jul-1999   Open 41.29 Hight 41.53 Low 40.51 Close 40.51 Volume 6.1M Chg -0-70 (-1.70%)

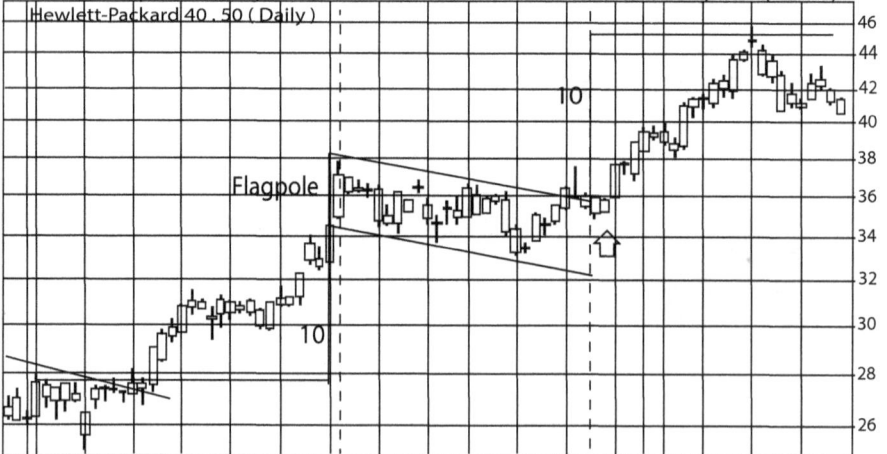

Hewlett-Packard 40 . 50 (Daily)

Flagpole

10

10

Reversal Price Patterns

Reversal price patterns are exactly what the name suggests. When you observe a price reversal pattern, it signals that the current trend direction will soon reverse. Let's take a look at the most popular reversal patterns for stock traders.

1. **Head and Shoulders**

A head and shoulders pattern can be signaling either a top reversal at the end of an upward trend or a bottom at the end of a downward price trend. This depends on where it occurs on the price chart.

When it comes to chart patterns, a picture speaks a million words. Here is an example of a classic head and shoulders pattern:

CENT Networks, Inc. (CENT) Nasdaq Nat. Mkt.
9-Jun-2000 **Open** 34.62 **High** 35.00 **Low** 33.75 **Close** 34.50 **Volume** 610.5k **Chg** +0.75 (+2.22%)

CENT Networks 34.50 (Dalily)

Head and Shoulders Reversal

Left Shoulder — Head — Right Shoulder

Neckline

Oct 98 Trendline

80 75 70 65 60 55 50 45 35 35 30 25

Aug Sep Oct Nov Dec 2000 Feb Mar Apr May Jun

Remember, head and shoulder patterns can also signal the end of a downward price trend.

Here's what a head and shoulders bottom looks like:

Alaska Air Group , Inc. (ALK) NYSE
10-Feb-1999 4:00pm Open 51.62 Hight 52.12 Low 51.31 Last 51.44 Volume 142.4K Chg -0.38 ▼

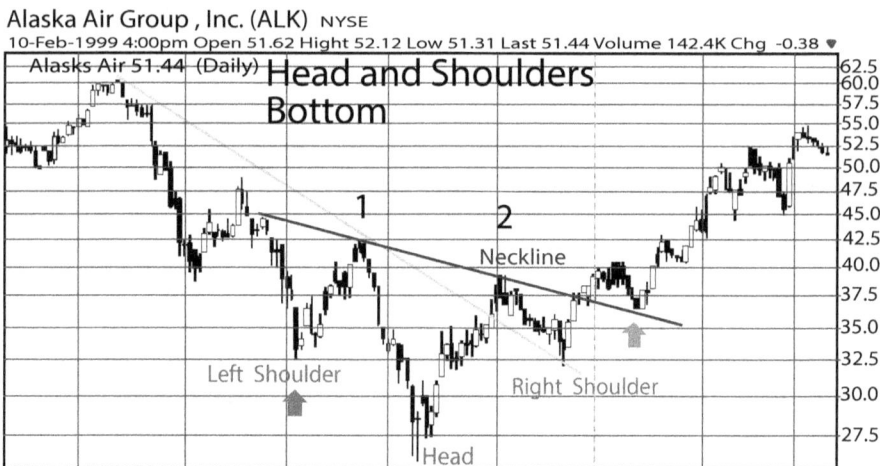

As you can see, the head and shoulder pattern signaling the bottom is exactly the opposite of the topping pattern.

2. **Rising and Descending Wedges**

Rising and Descending Wedge patterns are well-known reversal patterns found on financial charts. They are more open to interpretation than the double tops/bottoms. None the less, they can be significant reversal patterns that every chart reading technical analyst should understand.

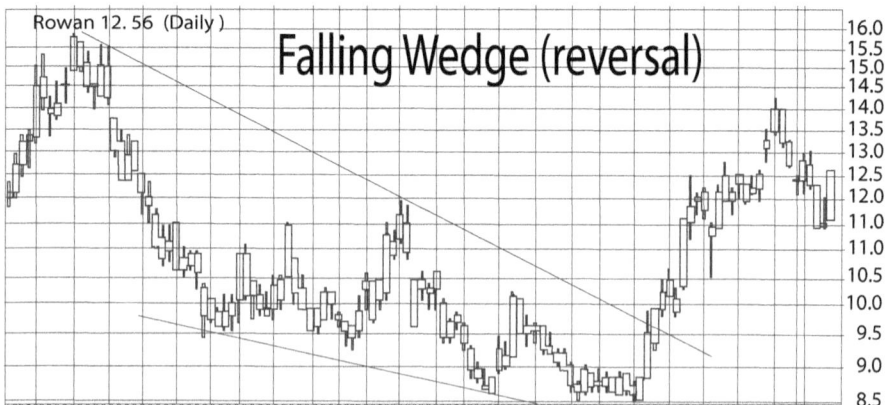

Dell Inc. (DELL)
2-Jan-2002   OP 27.60 HI 27.89 Lo 27.10 Cl 27.50 Vol 20.3M Chg +0.32 (+1.18%)
─PPO(12,26,9) 0.614, 1.501, -0.887 **Rising Wedge (reversal)**

Neg Diverge

¹⏐Dell 27. 50 (Daily)

3. Triple and Double Tops/Bottoms

Double and triple tops are essentially the same thing. The difference being the number of times the upper resistance level is tested. If its tested two times, it is a double top, three times, the formation becomes a triple top.

Rockwell Automation (ROK) NYSE
19-Nov-1999   Op 18.23 Hi 18.27 Lo 18.02 Cl 18.18 Vol 2.2M Chg -0.23

Triple Top (reverrsal)

3.2

3.2

Oct 98

By reversing this simple pattern after a downward trend, it becomes a double or triple bottom reversal pattern. Here's what it looks like:

Andrew Crop. (ANDW) Nasdaq Nat. Mkt
30-june-2000   Open 31.69 High 33.62 Low 31.4 Close 33.55 Volume 3.1M Chg +0.75 +2.06%

Support and Resistance

Support and resistance are terms describing price movements on a stock market price chart. Support and resistance are the basic building blocks of most forms of technical analysis. Understanding how to quickly identify support and resistance is a key to being a successful trader.

Knowing what support and resistance mean is critical for the understanding of stock charts. In fact, understanding technical indicators is often based on having a full understanding of support and resistance. This article will start from step one and explain support and resistance.

What are Support and Resistance?

Support and resistance are defined as areas on a stock price graph that appear to offer either support to dropping prices or resistance to price moving higher. Support and resistance are time frame dependent. This means that support on the hourly chart has nothing to do with support on a 15-minute stock graph.

A moving average or horizontal chart lines can be support and resistance.

Simple moving averages consist of a certain number of periods, averaged, then plotted as one point on a graph. For example, a 20 period simple moving average on a daily chart takes the last 20 days movement, adds it together, then divides by twenty to determine the average change during the time frame. The result is an upward or downward sloping line on the chart that acts as support or resistance.

Here's an example of the 50-day simple moving average that is acting as support and resistance

Horizontal support or resistance is a little harder to observe on a chart. The rudimentary definition is any price level that has been hit two or more times in the same direction that has either buttressed price from moving lower or kept the price from moving higher.

At the same time, a single period high or single session low can also become support or resistance. Every time price hits a support or resistance level and it acts as support or resistance the stronger the level is believed to be.

Lilly Eli & Co . (LLY) NYSE
2-Feb-2000 4:00pm   Open 63.65 High 64.20 Low 62.07 Last 63.23 Volume 2.1M Chg -0.49 ▼

In other words, support will become resistance and resistance will become support after being violated. While this is not something that you can bet the farm on, it does occur enough to make it worthwhile to keep it in mind while actively investing.

Volume

Volume is often referred to as the forgotten sister of price. Technical analysts define volume as the quantity of shares traded during a specified time frame. Sharp listeners would have noticed that volume is present on our pattern example charts. This is because the volume is what drives price. Without volume, price does not move.

Technical analysts utilize volume as a measure of the market and individual stock sentiment. The idea is that when a large number of shares are traded there is substantial interest in the stock. This can be either positive or negative interest depending on the direction of the prevailing trend.

Some traders use volume as a prediction tool. The basic rules of using volume as a prediction tool are as follows

1. If the price is upward trending and the volume is rising, prices will continue to advance.

2. If the price is down trending and the volume is falling, prices are expected to reverse.

3. If the price is down trending and volume is increasing, prices will continue to fall.

Remember, these are just rules of thumb for technical analysts. These rules are not set in stone, and there are many exceptions to the rules. To boil it down, you want to see volume increasing in the direction of the move. Should volume decline, it is a sure sign that the directional move may be coming to an end.

Also, should volume spike higher during a directional stock move, this may be signaling capitulation or the final surge of volume before price reverses. These volume spikes, although not perfect, can be an adamant signal that the price move is over.

While many traders are familiar with price and the stock market indicators derived from price, very few understand the stock market indicators tied to volume.

There is a saying that states, "Without volume price means nothing". What this means is that without understanding the price volume relationship, price alone does not provide enough clues to make wise trading decisions.

Here Are Two Volume Indicators You Need To Know

1. **On Balance Volume or OBV:**

This is among the most popular volume indicators used today.

It works to clarify if money is flowing into or out of a stock or contract.

The underlying theory is incredibly simple. A period of volume is added if the close is up and a period of volume is subtracted if the close is down.

These figures are charted to create the OBV line which is compared and contrasted to price find validations and deviations.

Fortunately, most of today's trading platforms include On Balance Volume as part of their technical analysis suite of tools. In addition, www.stockcharts.com is a great source for end of day OBV data and OBV daily and weekly charts.

Here's one way OBV looks when you actually use it for trading.

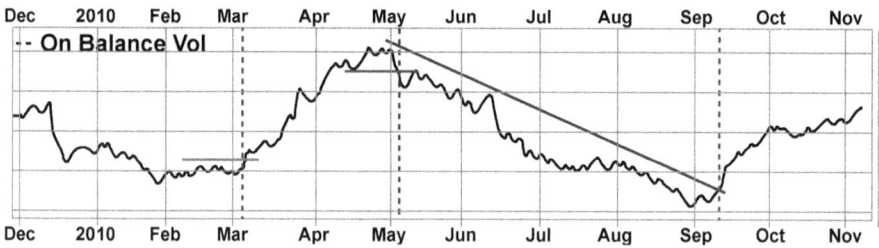

Here's a slightly different way to view the OBV indicator.

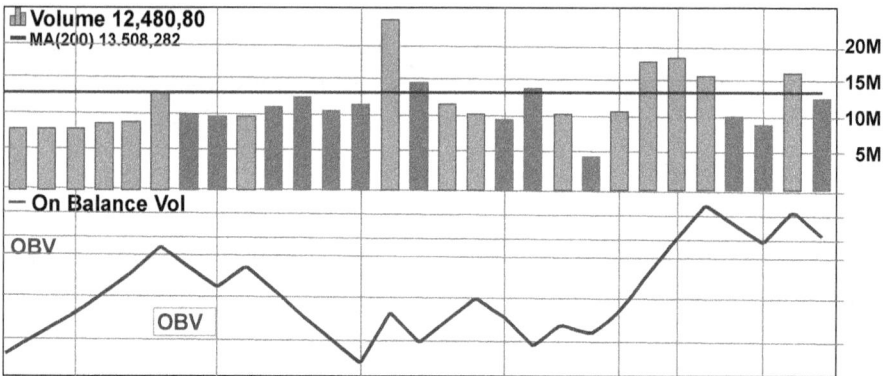

2. Accumulation/Distribution Line:

The A/D line was formulated by researcher Marc Chaiken. This tool is used to measure money flow into and out of stocks.

The primary difficulty with the A/D line is it does not illustrate a gap in price. A stock that gaps then closes within the range is not signaled with the A/D line.

This is why it is always critical to use these volume indicators in conjunction with price. Attempting to use the indicators as standalone tools is a recipe for disaster.

Here's an example of the Accumulation Distribution line:

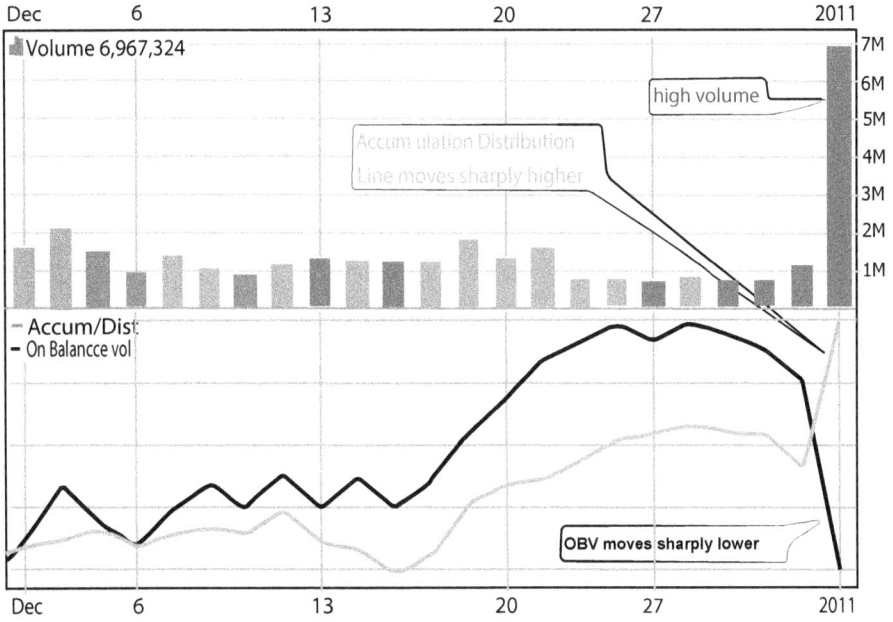

Here's another view with the line drawn behind the price bars.

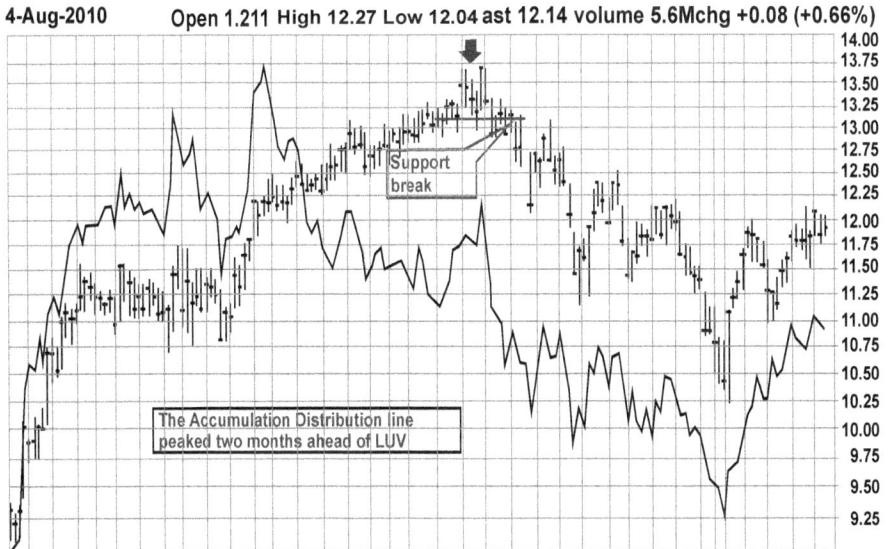

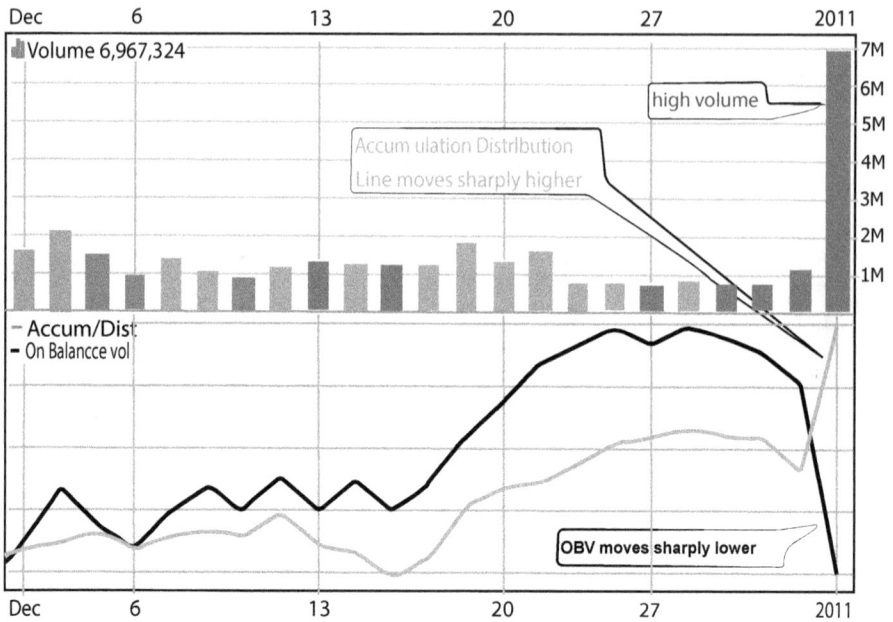

Chart labels (top axis): Dec 6 13 20 27 2011

Volume 6,967,324 — axis on right: 7M, 6M, 5M, 4M, 3M, 2M, 1M

high volume

Accumulation Distribution
Line moves sharply higher

– Accum/Dist
– On Balancce vol

OBV moves sharply lower

(bottom axis): Dec 6 13 20 27 2011

Alert readers will instinctively grasp the fact that these price patterns only exist after the fact. They are only visible on price charts after they form. This means that traders are forced to anticipate the pattern forming and take a position before the formation in most cases. Thereby proving that technical analysis is an intuitive, subjective art form and far from an objective science.

Viewing and attempting to use technical analysis as an objective science is a terrible lie of the market.

Technical Indicators

Technical traders use indicators to help clarify price. Indicators help eliminate the noise that is often inherent in a simple price chart to clarify trend. Let's take closer look at the most popular technical indicators.

Technical analysis is often made very complicated. Some investors just love to play with charts and create very sophisticated stock predictions. Well, believe it or not this is not how to make money. Keeping the stock chart as simple as possible is the key to successfully using stock market trends profitably. Most truly fruitful and profitable traders use only a handful of stock market indicators. Their favorites can be broken down into price smoothing indicators and leading indicators. Let's take a closer look:

The most fundamental of these is known as the **Simple Moving Average** or SMA. A Simple Moving Average determines the average price of a financial instrument over a specific number of periods.

Widely used time periods include 20, 50, and 200. These periods can be monthly, weekly, daily, hourly, 15 minutes, 5 minutes and 1 minute in duration. The longer the period the greater the significance of the SMA. Big money speculators and institutions often only focus on creating a self-fulfilling prophecy at times. The practical idea behind a moving average is that it smooth's data and makes it easier to define a trend.

It is important to note that one of the only academic studies indicating that technical analysis possesses an edge when making trading decisions was focused on the 200 days SMA and a long-term perspective in the stock market.

Price smoothing indicators, such as Simple Moving Averages follow price, **leading/momentum indicators** are believed to preceed price moves. In other words, the indicator is believed to predict price movements before their occurrence.

Momentum means the degree of change of a stock's price. The quicker the price moves, the more the momentum. As momentum drops, price often follows by dropping. The opposite is also true, increasing momentum usually goes hand in hand with rising prices.

One of the most prevalent momentum indicators is called the **Relative Strength Index** or RSI.

The Relative Strength Index or RSI contrasts the average price change of the advancing time frames with the average change of the declining periods.

RSI is an oscillating indicator first popularized by Welles Wilder in his 1978 book, "New Concepts In Technical Trading Systems". The standard period used by most technical analysts is fourteen.

The time frame is scaled on a chart from 0 to 100. Readings below 30 are believed to indicate an oversold condition; those above 70 are thought to indicate an overbought condition.

Here's an example of how RSI looks on the price chart:

WFR (MEMC Electronic Materials) NYSE
5-Oct-2009 4:00pm Op 15.63 Hi 15.90 Lo 15.36 Last 15.83 Vol 4.8m Chg +0.45 (+2.93%)

Here's another example:

MCD (Mcdonalds Corp.) NYSE
5-Mar-2008   Op 50.04 Hi50.35 Lo 49.52 Cl 50.14 Vol 7.6M Chg +0.29 (+0.58%)

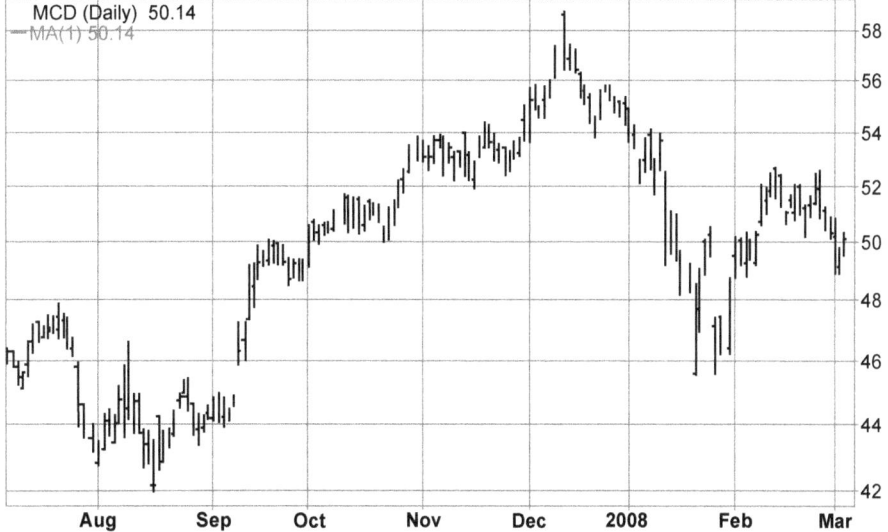

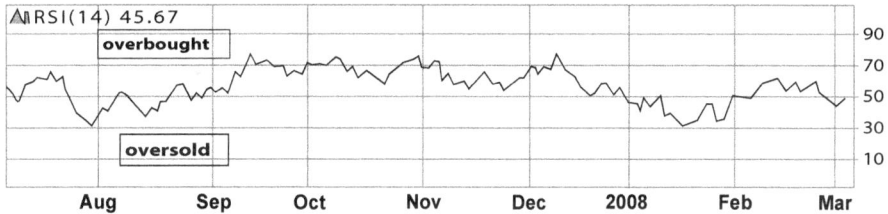

Understanding the TICK

The NYSE TICK indicator is a sentiment indicator that can provide an edge when properly used. The TICK is a second by second indicator that measures the number of NYSE stocks that have ticked upward minus those that have ticked downward. If the TICK reads 200 it means that 200 more stocks ticked higher than ticked lower in the last second of trade. If the TICK reads negative 200 it means that 200 more stocks moved lower than moved higher in the last second.

What I look for is extreme readings in the TICK. While the average range of the TICK is negative 400 to positive 400, it can move from negative 1000 to positive 1000. Whenever the TICK moves below negative 400, look for opportunities to buy the DJIA. By the same token, whenever the TICK moves above 400, look to short the DJIA.

When the TICK moves in either direction by 1000, it's time to ramp up the size of your positions in the opposite direction of the TICK.

ALWAYS REMEMBER:

Technical Analysis is far from a science and is an interpretive art form. As such, it is subjective and not objective. It is descriptive, not predictive. It cannot be properly objectively tested. So why do I include this information in the book? Despite its fatal flaws, TA provides a framework from which to make entry and exit decisions on individual trades. This in no way means that the structure provides an edge, but it does provide actionable levels from where to make decisions.

Chapter 14

Derivative Strategies To Beat The Machines

The world of options trading still contains viable edges for the individual trader. There are several derivative strategies that I have used effectively to earn consistent profits without regard to the HFT machines.

First, here are three benefits to using options to beat the machines.

1. **Flexibility**

Flexibility is the overriding theme for all options. Regardless of what you think is going to happen in the market, there is a derivative and/or strategy to implement. No matter what happens in the financial markets, there is a derivative tactic to exploit the situation.

2. **Leverage**

There is nothing worse than finding the perfect stock but not having enough capital to purchase or short it. Options allow undercapitalized traders to take advantage of situations otherwise inaccessible. With the proper use of options, even the smallest investor can control and benefit from expensive stocks.

If you are able to purchase stocks directly, options leverage creates the potential for much greater returns.

3. **Limits Risk**

I can hear some of you now, What the heck, options increase risk, not limit it, what is he talking about?!" Nothing could be further from the truth. Options were designed to limit and define risk. Remember, option buyers can only lose what they invested in the option. However, stock short sellers have theoretically unlimited downside risk since stocks can keep on climbing higher.

Also, certain strategies such as covered calls and selling puts can be used to limit risk in an existing portfolio.

Strategy # 1: How To Pay What You Want For Stocks

This tactic involves the selling of put options. Every put option represents 100 shares of stock. This means that for every 100 shares of stock that you want to purchase, at a certain price, you sell one put option at the strike price nearest the discount you want to buy the shares.

Only One of Two Things Can Happen

First, share price never drops to the strike price. If this happens, you get to keep the premium for selling the put option. Many winning investors make a very nice income by earning premium.

The second possible thing is that the stock falls to the strike price or below. If this happens, you will be "put" to the stock. In other words, required to purchase the shares at the discounted price already agreed, is the price where you want to own the shares.

The greatest news here is that you get to keep the premiums earned no matter what happens.

These premiums earned by selling the put will allow you to buy the stock by using even less of your money, therefore, in effect, getting an even steeper discount. Talk about a powerful strategy!

Many professional traders and investors use this strategy on a consistent basis. Collecting the premium and rarely being required to purchase the shares can be an effective strategy.

Managing The Worst Case (If you don't want to own the stock)

One difference between winning and losing traders is that the winners always think of what they can lose in every trade. Whereas, the losers only think about what they can win. With this said, in some situations, you may no longer want to purchase the stock at the strike price. This could be for reasons such as the fundamental picture of the stock has changed since you sold the put options.

If this occurs, you can buy back the put option at a loss.

Another reason you would buy back the puts at a loss would be a significant piece of bad news surfaces during the puts lifespan. This bad news will have long lasting effects on the stock, so it is best not to purchase the shares.

Derivative Strategy # 2 Collars

Recent volatility spikes such as the one experienced with Brexit make the critical importance of protecting your market gain to the forefront.

Black swan type events are occurring at an ever-faster frequency. Understanding how to protect your profits is critical to beat the machines over the long term.

Collars allows you to keep your winning stocks in an attempt to earn additional profits while protecting the downside at the same time.

The tactic is predominantly appealing if your stocks are dividend payers that you don't want to dump but are fearful that the share price is moving lower.

The tactic is known as an Option Collar.

Collars are simple to use and understand derivative tactic. Collars are implemented by stockholders trying to control the downside risk of a profitable stock position at little or no cost.

Believe it or not, collars can sometimes be built to create profits for the trader.

What Is A Derivative Collar?

A derivative collar is the simulatanious buying of a put option and the selling/writing of a call option.

Both the put and call are out of the money and generally have the identical expiration date.

For every 100 shares of stocks that you wish to protect the profits yet hold onto the shares, one put is purchased and one call is sold.

For example, if you want to protect 1000 shares of ABC, a collar would consist of purchasing 10 put options and writing 10 call options to protect all 500 shares.

If you believe you need three months of protection against a plunge in the shares, the derivitives making up the collar should have a three month or longer expiration date.

The collar tactic is perfect for investors seeking a risk adverse method to earn a realistic rate of return while controling downside risk potential.

The key to being effective with collars is picking the appropriate put and call combination permitting upside while managing the downside risk.

The most appealing aspect of this strategy is that the combination can be rolled from month to month earning a potential 3-5% monthly return if the stock price moves as expected.

Rolling refers to the tactic of repurchasing the short calls while writing new calls for another month and sometimes different strike price, and purchasing fresh puts for the collar.

Repeating simply, fine-tuning the collar to fit the price of the stock in that particular month.

This is a very common stratagem among professional option traders. Many earn their living doing this consistently.

Another interest factoid is corporate executives utilize this tactic to defend their capital when it is concentrated in the company's stock. The collar guards the executive's wealth without demanding the expense of pricey put only protection.

Are not options costly insurance? Why are collars relatively cheap or even free?

The reason collars are cheap or even free downside protection, is due to the premium earned from the call options being utilized to pay the purchase price of the protective put options.

You can sometimes launch the collar at no cost since the premium earned is greater than the price of the purchased option, the collar is called a **zero-cost collar**.

Interestingly, collars can also produce returns. Income producing collars are widely believed to be more conservative than cheap or zero cost collars.

Income producing collars are structured by purchasing a put and the writing of a call with the call strike price with the strike prices close together. This lower strike price creates cash greater than that required to pay for the put.

The downside is that it limits the upside potential of the stock. It is also critical not to forget commissions and other fees imposed by your broker when considering such strategies.

Also, always keep in mind the tax implications of trading options and check with a qualified tax expert. Finally, it is important to read the CBOE's Risk Disclosure statement if you are new in the option game.

Chapter 15

Choosing The System

This is where everything comes together. Your stock trading system will allow you to choose the right stocks and provide you with high probability entries and exits for actively trading these stocks.

The most successful traders use a combination of Price Driver and technical analysis to create profitable stock trading systems.

I like to use the fundamental information to choose the specific stocks to trade then screen for technical signals to time entries and exits. Always keep in mind the inexact nature of technical analysis! However, it does provide a price based framework from which to make timing decisions.

Fundamental Screening Criteria:

My favorite and perhaps the most useful fundamental screening system of all time is called CANSLIM.

William O'Neil is one of the most famous stock pickers of all time. He is credited with pioneering the use of computers for analyzing stocks. O'Neil became famous as the publisher of Investor's Business Daily and the author of "How to Make Money in Stocks: A Winning System in

Good Times and Bad". Fashioned after an comprehensive study of eight different market cycles over 40 years of data, O'Neil identified seven different factors that all the top performing companies possessed. He named this investing tactic CANSLIM, with each letter of the word representing one of the seven success factors for stock growth.

CANSLIM has stood the test of time with the American Association of Individual Investors ranking it as the best portfolio strategy with a ten-year average return of 13.2%.

I like the fact that the strategy is not a one trick pony relying on a single niche stock analysis technique. CANSLIM combines both technical and fundamental factors when choosing companies for investment. It covers all the bases for what creates a winning stock.

Here is what CANSLIM stock-picking method represents:

C = Current Earnings

The method searches for companies with strong, increasing quarterly earnings. Minimum increases of 18 to 20% over the same quarterly period year over year are a must for the company to pass the screening.

A= Annual Earnings Increases

Yearly earnings need to be increasing from year to year. The average earning rate expected is 21% overall.

N= New Products, New Management, New Highs

These are the fundamental trigger that pushes stocks to new highs. Fluctuations in the company's products and management often precede an increase in share price. Firms with new goods and/or switching management can be difficult for non-insiders to know about as it is happening. Therefore, using technical analysis to screen for stocks making new highs may reveal information before the information before released.

S= Supply and Demand

O'Neil discovered that 95% of the winning stocks had fewer than 25 million shares outstanding. This is due to the share price of companies with a smaller share float increasing faster than companies with a larger float. The traditional economic law of supply & demand.

L= Laggard or Leader

Laggard or Leader refers to the relative strength of the company when compared with others in its segment. Canslim teaches to only purchase stocks with relative strength grades of 80 or 90%.

I = Institutional Ownership

Institutional ownership is a crucial aspect with CANSLIM. The stock must be owned by a minimum of three major institution

M= Market Direction

Finally, O'Neil states to only use the CANSLIM strategy when the overall market is up trending. He teaches to determine this condition by watching the indexes for overall market direction.

Taking losses is a critical part of the CANSLIM method. Once the position has fallen 8 to 10% from the entry level, take the loss. This proactive move serves two purposes. First, it will help mitigate losses and second you will be able to redeploy the capital into new shares.

Obviously, CANSLIM is not the only way to fundamentally screen for profitable stocks. In fact, the internet is full of fundamental stock screeners that can be tweaked to nearly any criteria.

My Favorite Free Fundamental Stock Screens

1. MY FAVORITE FREE OVERALL STOCK SCREENER

Finviz.com is my favourite comprehensive fundamental/technical stock screener that's available for free. It provides a wide variety of data points that can be selected for filtering data.

2. MY FAVORITE FREE SURPRISE/REVISION SCREENER

Earnings surprises and revisions are key factors that fundamentally move stock prices. History has proven that a company's stock has a tendency to rise after reporting earnings that are higher than analyst estimates. Zacks.com provides an excellent screener for earnings.

3. MY FAVORITE FREE MUTUAL FUND SCREENER

Morningstar.com by far provides the top free screening system for mutual funds. Yes, I understand that you are an active trader and not a buy and hold mutual fund player. Well, the truth is that maverick traders no matter how active you are, its best to trade around core investment positions. Mutual funds can make ideal core investment for everyone's portfolio.

4. MY FAVORITE FREE ETF SCREENER

ETF's or Exchange Traded Fund provide every stock trader the ability to trade commodities, indexes, currencies and sectors in a simple transaction, just like buying a single stock. ETF's have become exceedingly popular, often crushing individual stocks in terms of volume. The top ETF screener is Etfdb.com. You can sort the entire ETF universe by a number of data fields, including expense ratio, market return, beta, and dividend yield.

5. MY FAVORITE POPULAR STOCK SCREENER

The advent of social media has opened up an entire new avenue for stock pickers. Sites such as www.stocktwits.com and www.seekingalpha. com have features to help you locate the communities' hot stocks at any time. The Motley Fool rates stocks on a 1-5 scale based on the "outperform" and "underperform" votes of its 74,000 users. The more users that vote a stock "outperform," the higher the stock's rating and vice versa. While this screening method is questionable, it is important to note that there have been several hedge funds launched that rely on this data to make decisions.

FUNDAMENTAL SCREENING PARAMETERS

Many investors prefer to screen fundamentally with their own parameters to locate trading opportunities. While these methods can vary, on average, they all contain the same basic parameters.

These parameters were first popularized by the top performing mutual fund manager of all time Fidelity Investment's Peter Lynch.

Lynch discovered that certain fundamental metrics seemed to be a constant in all winning stocks. Here are his basic criteria for building a stock selection system.

1. **Market Cap**

Stocks with a market capitalization under $5 billion are believed to have greater upside potential than giant entrenched companies. This is because these relatively small firms are hungry for market share and are often on a growth trajectory. Obviously, there are exceptions to this rule, but overall it makes sense.

2. **PEG Ratio Below 1.2**

The PEG ratio relates a company's price-earnings ratio with its projected growth rate. A PEG ratio of 1 indicates that a company is fairly valued. As the PEG ratio moves higher than 1, the company becomes progressively overvalued. At the same time, a PEG ratio below one reveals an undervalued company.

3. **15 to 30% Earnings Growth**

This is a five year average growth rate that is ideal for a growing company. Companies that exceed 30% often have difficulty sustaining such rapid growth. In addition, stocks with such a high growth rate are often very popular and have already seen this reflected in the stock price. This goes along with Lynch's idea of only investing in less popular stocks and avoids the super popular names.

4. **Debt Ratio under 35%**

A debt to equity ratio below 35% indicates that a company's debt ratios are not excessive. Excessive debt makes expansion difficult as the debt weighs heavily on the company. Not to mention the problems obtaining additional growth financing when burdened with excessive debt.

5. **Institutional Ownership between 5 and 65%**

It's critical that institutions have interest in your stock. These big money players have a vested interest in helping to support the stocks that they own and it's smart to have them on your side. Believe it or not, stocks that have the lower level of institutional interest often have the best growth potential. This is because, once institutions start buying shares, the price could easily rocket higher. In other words, getting into the stock before the institutions notice it is key.

Now that we understand the basic fundamental screening criteria, the next step is how to enter trades into the stocks that pass the fundamental screens.

Chapter 16

Entry Signals

This is where the rubber hits the road. All the Price Driver theory and picking the strongest stock are for naught if the entry signal is not effective. The entry signal is how the trade is entered. It consists of the criteria needed to be fulfilled before actually buying or shorting the stock.

This is where technical analysis comes into play. Technical analysis allows you to pinpoint the exact time for you to subjectively enter and exit trades. Although these tactics can be used successfully to trigger trades, they are far from fool proof on a case by case basis. Remember, finding success as an active trader is a process. In other words, success is measured over a series of trades rather than any single trade. This means that, when combined with the earlier Price Driver metrics, these entry signals triggers provide the structure needed to trigger trades. With that said, let's get started with a few entry signals.

The Break Out Entry Signal

The breakout strategy is among the most popular entry strategies for trading. It is accessible and far easier to execute mentally than pullback tactics.

The basic idea of a breakout strategy is that the trader identifies a pattern, range or channel then patiently waits for the price to "breakout" and buys or sells in the direction of the break.

The theory being that the directional momentum will continue, carrying your trade into profitable territory. The reason it works is many other traders may be waiting for the same break out.

Once the breakout occurs, they all jump onboard pushing your position to profits.

My favorite breakout strategy is called the "Death Channel Break Out."

Use a fifteen-minute bar chart. Identify the high and low of the first 15-minute bar formed on the chart. I call this channel the Death Channel since the daily direction can be very uncertain within it.

Next switch to a 3-minute graph with the high and low of the first 15 minute drawn with horizontal lines on the chart. Now is the time for patience. Wait for a full 3-minute bar to close above the upper line, or an entire 3-minute red candle to cross the lower line to go short.

I like using trailing stops after the positions are in profits. Prior to profits being earned, use the original entry lines or slightly below to prevent sharp losses when the breakout fails to have momentum.

Every trader has their own criteria for entering trades with the break out system. The system works great when the stock or market is trending in one direction or another. However, when the market or stock is choppy, it will result in many false entries and stop outs.

The Death Channel system calls for trying the entry at the breakout levels three times before the level is discarded as being false.

Price often pushes higher and falls back several times before the final breakout. I have found that three entry attempts and stop outs at the breakout line are usually enough to say confidently that the breakout did not work, and it is time to look for another entry level or instrument. Some traders expect these breakouts to fail, hence short near where breakout traders is going long.

The 15-minute initial time frame is for day traders. Those with longer time horizons can use longer term bars to build the Death Channel.

5 Steps To The Death Channel Breakout On A Daily Time Frame

Here are the five simple steps for trading the Death Channel

Step 1. Mark a recent high on the daily chart

Step 2. Draw a horizontal line at this high

Step 3. Simply wait for a full bar to close above this line (this is the break out)

Step 4. Enter long with the line now acting as the initial stop level.

Step 5. As price moves in your direction, move the stop level, based on your risk tolerance and goals, to lock in profits.

Remember, step one does not necessarily need to be the daily high. The break out line can be drawn at the simple moving average or other technical resistance patterns. The daily high is just one example of how to use the breakout strategy. Also, should price breakout of the lower Death Channel line, the system calls for a short entry.

MCD (Mcdonalds Corp.) NYSE
5-Mar-2008   Op 50.04 Hi50.35 Lo 49.52 Cl 50.14 Vol 7.6M Chg +0.29 (+0.58%)
MCD (Daily) 50.14
MA(1) 50.14
The Channel Trading System
Enter long on a break of this line
Enter short on a break of this line

```
$INDU (Daily) 17685.73
─MA(50) 17043.39
─MA(200) 16715.96        Buy on a break out ⬆    Short on a break down ⬇
dlVolume 286,040,512
```

Channel and another breakout tactics are the backbones of a trading strategy known as trend following or turtle trading. Turtle trading has been made accessible by author Michael Covel in his books **Trend Following** and **Turtle Trader**. I strongly recommend checking out Michael's trend books even if you are not a trend trader!

Turtle Soup Entry

I bring this idea up here because one of the most efficient entry methods I have ever used is called **Turtle Soup**. This entry method was popularized by hedge fund manager Linda Bradford Raschke and market researcher/author Larry Connors. While originally designed for commodities traders, this entry process can be uncannily powerful for stock trading.

The name comes from the popular turtle trading strategy that is basically a break out buying trading tactic. Investors who understand stock charts and understand technical indicators know that breakouts often fail. This is a fact of the stock market. The Turtle Soup tactic profits from failed breakouts. Let's take a closer look.

Every trader has experienced this losing situation. Finally, after what felt like forever, the share price breaks above the resistance level and your order is filled. You sit back in your chair waiting for the anticipated momentum performs exactly how you expect.

Immediately, your feelings of pleasure and accomplishment turn to dread and fear. The break out has failed and price is plunging. Since you were so confident in the break out, you completely forgot to have a stop loss order ready and waiting for such a scenario. At first you feel frozen convinced that if you just wait a few more minutes price will surely bounce back, at least to break even so you can get out without much of a loss.

Next, the fear of greater losses steps into your mind and you just sit there like a deer frozen in the headlights of an oncoming car.

Soon, the stock has fallen several points and you finally close the position completely exhausted and disgusted at yourself. You swear you will never let this happen again as you start searching the market for the next opportunity.

Just what happened, why didn't the trade work out?

The above scenario has happened to everyone who has ever attempted to trade the stock market. The market action is called a variety of names, some of which are too graphic to mention! The most common terms used to describe this occurrence are "fake out," "false breakout," and "head fake."

The cause of this very unfortunate, but all too common market action is usually the big money hedge funds, institutions, and even large traders selling into strength. You see these folks generally cannot just sell at a whim. Their trade size is such that they have to wait for high liquidity to sell their shares at the best price at the time.

Therefore, they sell into strength or break outs.

Interestingly, many of these head fakes correlate to round numbers, triple zeros, and areas of double, triple or more tops on the stock chart.

The reason being is that the big money professionals KNOW where retail (who they often call "the paper") have their buy orders set. While break outs can work as expected, it's critical that you always have stop loss orders in place to prevent taking a large loss.

The way I use the Turtle Soup tactic is I immediately reverse short when the breakout fails and falls back. Shorting in this manner often catches multiple points of profit.

Pull Back Entries

There is no question that buying weakness and selling strength works in the stock market. However, this is the most difficult thing to do psychologically.

Losing traders make the mistake of chasing sharp upward moves in stocks. Bullish news hits the news wire, and shares immediately take off to the upside. This is because institutions and many professional traders have real time news scanning software that will immediately alert them to the news before it filters into most affordable retail trader's news services.

Not to mention the fact that when the actual bullish news hits the wire, shares often sell off due to the sell the facts, buy the rumor phenomenon.

Also, even if the upward move triggered by the bullish news lasts several sessions, it is near impossible to tell when it will end. Remember, the same big money traders who pushed the stock higher are the ones who will take profits sending shares lower.

Due to the always uncertain nature of the markets, nothing is sure. With this said, often waiting for the first pullback to go long after a sharp upward move is an ideal way to enter the trade.

Remember, the goal is to be on the same side of the move as the big money, professional traders. When the initial push higher ends, it is generally due to the pro's taking profits. The professionals will then wait until the stock reaches enough of a discounted price before buying it again thus pushing it higher.

The smartest way to approach a pull back is a set of rules. These rules can vary. Sometimes they can call for a duration such as three days; sometimes they are based on how sharp the pullback, other times it relies on technical support levels derived from Fibonacci or other esoteric technical analysis techniques. I have found that all these methods work sometimes and sometimes they do not.

When I used to work for Larry Connor's at Trading Markets and CG3, a very effective method for buying pullbacks was developed and successfully tested. The method consisted of the following rule set.

1. **The price must be above the 200-day simple moving average.**

This is the line in the sand that differentiates a stock that is likely to bounce back or continue lower. Going long a stock that is trading below its 200-day simple moving average is simply too risky to create a strong risk-reward ratio for the entry.

2. **Screen for stocks that have fallen for five or more days consecutively**

Stocks that have dropped for five or more days, yet are above the 200-day simple moving average, have proven statistically to outperform the market over the short term.

3. **Wait for the first higher close on the daily chart to buy.**

This confirms that shares are being bought. Yes, you will miss some of the upsides but the safety net created by waiting often outweighs the potential theoretical gains of catching the upward move from its start. No one knows when the buying will start again. This is why waiting for it makes trading sense.

The VIX Stretch Entry

Using correlated instruments combined with proven entry tactics to time entries into the stock indexes is a time proven way to beat the machines. One of my favorite correlated entry triggers is known as the VIX Stretch.

When I worked with Larry Connors at Trading Markets, we tested this entry method and discovered 84.85 % of the 33 trades taken being profitable. An average of 363.90 SPX points were earned with an average hold time of 5 trading sessions. We first published this system in article format at Trading Markets. Here is a brief recap.

The Volatility Index or VIX was initially used in1993. The index is constructed based on a paper published by Dr. Robert Whaley.

The VIX document implied volatility of the S&P 500 over the next month. It utilizes a weighted mix of prices for a series of options on the S&P 500.

The options are valued based on the expected volatility or price changes over the following 30 days.

The VIX formula is the square root of the par variance swap rate for the next 30 days. An easy to understand and useable way to visualize the VIX is the reading reflects the expected percentage move of the S&P 500 over the next 30 days on an annualized basis. This reading has been as little as 9% and as high as 89% since the VIX was launched.

The VIX is a contrary indicator. This means that when markets drop the VIX usually climbs demonstrating fear with the change in option prices.

Bullish markets generally create a lower VIX as fear exits the market and greed takes a pivotal role. As an example, in October 2008, the VIX hit its all-time high corresponding with the sharp market decline.

Now that we understand how the VIX works, how can you apply this knowledge to help your trading? The best way to view the VIX is as a dynamic and not static indicator. Viewing the VIX statically is the primary mistake traders make when trying to build VIX systems.

VIX Stretches is one highly profitable system for trading the stock market indexes, namely the S&P 500.

The concept is the longer the VIX remains higher than its 10 period Moving Average, and the higher it is above this average, the better the odds of a market rally. We further quantified this idea by breaking it into a 3 step system to properly test the results. Here is how we did it.

1. The SPY is trading above its 200 day SMA

2. The VIX is stretched 5% higher than its 10 day SMA for 3 or more days. If so, buy the market on the close.

3. The trade is closed when the SPY closes above a RSI(2) reading of 65 or more

Chapter 17

Worst Case Stop Loss

No matter how carefully you choose your entry. Regardless of having all the statistics, fundamentals and odds in your favor for a winning trade, sometimes it just doesn't work out, and the stock moves in the opposite direction. No matter how robust and profitable your trading system, you are going to have losses. Believe it or not, even professional big money traders have losses. Often professionals take multiple losses in a row.

Sometimes this adverse move can be sharp and severe. In fact, it's often so fast that you don't have the time to react to close the trade. This can occur during an overnight event that causes the stock to gap lower or any severe event during the trading day.

This is why a worst-case stop loss is a must for every trade. I am not talking about mental stop losses, or even stop loss levels written down in your trading plan. I am talking about a hard set stop loss set on your trading platform.

Where this worst-case stop loss is set is up to you and your risk tolerance. My suggestion to you, since this is a worst-case stop loss is that it is set at 26% away from your entry point on the stock.

Here is an example. If you purchase a stock at $100.00 per share, setting your worst-case stop loss at $74.00 makes sense. With that said,

I like to avoid double zero numbers when setting stop losses. This is because shares appear to have a tendency to reverse at a double zero number. Therefore, setting this stop loss at $73.93 would be ideal.

Another common way to set the worst-case stop loss is below a technical resistance level. This level could be the 200 day simple moving average, a long term low, or whatever technical pattern you feel comfortable using. The problem with not having a fixed percentage and using a technical level instead is that it is not as quantifiable as using a fixed percentage each time. However, it really depends on what you are most comfortable using and your risk tolerance.

Let's take a closer look at the three primary types of stop loss orders.

1. **Sell-Stop Order**

This protects your long positions by triggering a market sell order when the price falls below your preset limit. In the above example, a market order would be triggered when the price falls below $73.93 per share.

2. **Buy –Stop Order**

These orders are the same thing as Sell Stop Orders except they are used to protect short positions in the stock market. In other words, a market order is triggered once the price rises above the set level.

3. **Stop – Limit Order**

Stop Limit orders work in the same manner as Sell or Buy Stop orders. However, instead of a market order being triggered, a limit order is triggered. This allows the trader to have complete control over the price that the trade is executed. However, at the same time, during fast or volatile conditions, the limit order may not be filled. This is a distinct risk of using Stop Limit orders.

My favorite way to determine where to set stop loss orders is by using an idea known as Average True Range.

Average True Range ATR is a technical analysis tool created by Welles Wilder and popularized in his book, "New Concepts in Technical Trading Systems" in 1978.

ATR measures a stocks or futures volatility and not the direction, strength or length of a move.

By volatility, I mean specifically how much does the stock or future move in a given period, its price range. ATR is the average of the TrueRange.

True Range is the greatest of the current low and previous close, the difference between the present high and the previous close, or the difference between the current low and the previous close. The average of the TrueRange is then calculated over a set number of periods to determine the ATR.

The number of periods used is generally 14. A high ATR number means the price is moving a lot during the period, a low ATR means the price is not moving much.

That is all the ATR tells you. How can such a tool be used by traders.

I primarily use the ATR as a method of setting stops. I determine the ATR of a stock/future, times it by 3, and then subtract this number from my entry price to determine where to set my stop.

This tries to eliminate being stopped out on non-significant movements that are within the average price range of the stock. Also, it provides enough play in the price so that your stop is well outside of the erratic gyrations or price noise of the stock/future.

Once your trade is profitable by above the ATR, ATR can also be used to set profit taking exits.

Profit Taking Exits

This is the polar opposite of stop losses. Profit taking exits are used to close positions that are in profits. Without taking the profit and converting it into cash, the gains remain unrealized. Only by selling your shares do you make the turn the profits into the reality of cash. There is a multitude of profit taking exit strategies.

Here are my favorites:

1. **Trailing Stop Loss**

This is by far my favorite exit technique. Fortunately, most stock trading platforms have this feature built in so that it can be set without having to be monitored on the minute-by-minute basis.

As stated, a trailing stop loss moves in the direction of the stock. In other words, it is set so that the order maintains a set distance from price as the price moves in your direction.

Let's imagine you purchased shares at $25.00 per share. Soon, the price jumps to $30.00 per share creating a handsome profit. However, you do not want to close the trade yet as you firmly believe that, the stock will be going higher.

The ideal move in this situation would be to set a trailing stop to follow around $2.50 behind the share price. This means that you are locking in profits no matter what happens to price.

Let's say price immediately starts to reverse aggressively, the stop loss would be triggered at $27.50 per share locking in $2.50 of profits. Now, let's imagine that price continues moving higher. At $40.00 per share, the stop loss would have automatically moved to $37.50. Isn't that the coolest thing? I love trailing stops! It is a powerful tool.

2. **Price Target Exits**

Some successful traders like to set price targets for exits. Think of price targets as the opposite of stop loss orders. The sell order is executed once the upper price level is hit. Profit targets are very useful for short-term day trading since they can be set automatically to take small consistent profits during the trading day. This frees up your time to search for more opportunities. I do not like target price exits, for most of my trading, since it limits the upside. However, forshort-term day traders, it makes sense.

3. **Technical Exits**

There is a variety of technically based profit taking exit strategies. This means to exit on individual technical events such as making an all time high or falling below resistance. Using the Average True Range is my personal favorite technically based profit taking exit method.

Chapter 18

Position Sizing

Now we are getting into one of the most crucial ideas behind being a winning trader. Position sizing means how many shares to purchase based on your active trading account size. The skill of proper position sizing can mean the difference between a very profitable year and a year with disappointing results.

Position sizing is best understood by example.

Let's assume you have $100,000.00 in your account dedicated to active trading. You want to trade a stock that is trading for $10.00 per share. Your position-sizing limit for this volatile stock is 1% of your account size. This means that you can buy 100 shares of the stock at $10.00 per share. If your position size rules dictate 3%, you can then purchase 300 shares of the $10.00 per share stock.

This is the difference between traders and just someone who gambles in the stock market. The gambler will risk 20, 30, 50% or even more on a single trade idea. The true professional maverick trader knows better. He or she would never risk more than what their pre-set rules determined for the stock.

Position size can vary depending on market conditions, the individual stock volatility, and your risk tolerance levels. These numbers are not set in granite, but a good rule of thumb is never to risk over 5% on even your best trading ideas.

This value that you will risk is called R in financial circles. R is calculated by account size and the percentage of the account you will risk on the trade. Using R enables the trader to set stop losses and position size correctly while never risking more than the pre-determined amount of the trade.

Remember, with an R of 1% of your total account; you can be wrong five times in a row and still only lose 5% of your account. The key to success is not to lose your capital. Capital is your tool to make more money. Proper position sizing helps ensure that you will never suffer a catastrophic trading loss that knocks you out of the game.

Now it's time to drill down into the primary investing strategies. These are long-term strategies that enable you to slowly build wealth over time. The two primary strategies are value and growth investing. While both these techniques have the same goal of creating profits in the stock market, the way they go about it is very different when it comes to stock selection. Let's take a closer look:

Chapter 19

Value Investing Heroes

We talked about value investing earlier in the book. Now it is time to take deeper look.

Value investing is championed by the greatest investors who have ever walked the earth. Names like Warren Buffett, Charles Munger and Mario Gabelli are strong proponents of value investing.

Value investing, at its core, is locating and investing in stocks that are underpriced relative to their actual intrinsic value. In other words, it's the search for bargains in the universe of stocks.

Value investing is among the most popular stock picking strategies. It seeks to find stocks that are underpriced based on their intrinsic value. Value investors search for stocks that have strong fundamentals but whose price is indicating a bargain. The idea being that price will catch up to the actual value of the company providing the savvy value investor profits.

It is crucial that you grasp the difference between value and stock price.

The two have very little to do with each other at times. Value is the intrinsic worth of the company. High-quality companies with long track records and popular products/services have a high intrinsic value. Companies with high stock prices but weak fundamentals are not value companies. Many high-tech and internet type firms fall into this, not value category.

Warren Buffett preaches a great way to think about buying value stocks. I have found this method to be excellent. The method is to realize you are buying a business and not just the stock. The value investor sees him or herself as a company owner and not just a shareholder. It is through the lens of a business owner that a value investor chooses stocks. Value investors do not pay attention to daily fluctuations or market volatility.

I can hear what you are thinking now. Enough of the theory, show us how actually to locate profit-making value stocks! I have broken down the value stock picking method to seven easy to follow keys to screening.

Every investing strategy has its rules of conduct or guidelines. Value investing is no different. Here are five rules for value investing success.

1. **Solid Dividend Yield**

A solid dividend yield that has been increasing over the last several years is key to locating stocks with long-term value. I like to see a minimum of five years of dividend increases.

2. **Assets Greater Than Liabilities**

While this may sound obvious, it is critical that you check the balance sheet of any investment to make certain the company is not upside down, and that assets out number liabilities. Debt kills value, and high debt is a definite no-no when it comes to picking value stock

3. **Debt must be lower than equity**

This clear guideline is often missed by investors, yet is a must in choosing a winning value stock.

4. **The stock price must be higher than the Tangible Book Value**

A stock cannot be overpriced relative to the book value to be considered a value stock. Avoid any stock whose stock price is greater than the tangible book value.

5. **PEG Can Not Be Greater Than One**

A PEG greater than one can be a warning sign that the value is not as it appears. This rule can be bent a little at times if the rest of the metrics are supportive of value. Investors can go up to a 1.5 PEG ratio and still see value in the shares.

Mario Gabelli's Value Investing Secret:

Mario Gabelli is the real king of value investors. Using a dominant value plus a catalyst stock picking methodology that has been described as, *Graham Dodd + Warren Buffet = Gabelli*, his fund GAMCO has returned an after fee average return of nearly 12% per year for the past quarter of a century. These solid, steady gains have made Gabelli a billionaire who manages over $40 billion in client assets.

He uses a research-driven approach to investing taking into consideration free cash flow minus the expenditures needed to grow the business and earnings per share trends.

Gabelli's secret to value investing success can be diluted down to two terms. Private Market Value (PMV) and Catalyst.

PMV is the value an informed industrialist would pay to purchase an asset with similar characteristics. *(Astute readers will note the similarity between this and Buffett's teaching of treating a stock as a company)*

PMV is Calculated by studying on and off balance sheet assets, liabilities, as well as, free cash flow. Gabelli next compares these numbers with actual transactions in similar businesses as a reality check. Columbia Business School credits him with inventing the concept of PMV. In other words, he focuses on companies that appear to be bargains about their PMV. This provides Gabelli with upside potential plus a wide margin of safety.

After determining the stock is undervalued about its PMV, Gabelli looks for a pending catalyst to surface the value. He teaches that the catalyst can be anything. Examples are a company or industry specific happening such as a change in management, as pin-off, regulatory changes, or industry consolidation.

Gabelli's goal is to identify companies that have the potential of 50% return over the next 24 months. Once a particular stock reaches its Private Market Value, or if an expected catalyst fails to occur, Gabelli sells the stocks. It is all a very regimented process at GAMCO.

Summing it up, Gabelli invests in value stocks with high PMV and a pending catalyst that will force the share price to reflect the true value. This active approach to value investing is very research intensive but the results speak for themselves.

A Funny Story About Mario Gabelli.

I am fortunate enough to be friends with several of Mario Gabelli's seed investors. Several years ago, I was lucky enough to be invited by my friend Alexander to attend GAMCO's annual investor meeting in New York City. Alexander's father was a very early investor in GAMCO and received real VIP treatment at the meeting.

We were sat at a table of honor with the top brass at GAMCO. About half way through the meeting, right before it was time to meet and chat with Mr. Gabelli, I became very ill. Fighting to hold in my meal, I finally could not hold it in any longer and sprinted to the exit door. It was literally seconds prior to meeting Mario! Much to the chagrin of the hotel, the contents of my stomach were spewed all over the beautiful hall way and wall just outside the ballroom, not to mention all over my new suit. Fortunately, I was able to avoid hitting Mr. Gabelli or anyone else with my stomach bile.

Embarrassed and not smelling the best, I ran to my hotel room to change. I never returned to the meeting and would like to use this time to apologize publicly to Alexander and Mr. Gabelli!

Chapter 20

Growth Investing Heroes

Just like value investing, growth investing deserves a deeper look.

Many ultra successful hedge fund managers are hard-core growth investors. However, perhaps the most well known, and successful growth investors are Peter Lynch from Fidelity Investments. Lynchis known for being the manager of Fidelity's Magellan Fund, which was the top performing stock-based mutual fund of all time. As we stated earlier, growth investing and value investing have the same goals but the way each goes about reaching the goal are radically different.

Peter Lynch is among the most famous and fruitful investors alive. Active long before the hedge fund titans and their investments for the ultra high net worth individuals took center stage; Lynch focused on the middle-class investor. Best known for managing the top performing mutual fund of all time, Fidelity's Magellan Fund, his specialty is growth investing.

Often believed to be the opposite of value investing which focuses on the beat down stocks with high intrinsic value. Growth investing seeks out good news, expanding earnings, and other bullish impetuses that will push shares even higher. In other words, growth investing speculates that right things will get better.

Peter Lynch used several, at the time, secret tactics for choosing the right growth stocks for his mutual fund. Here they are:

1. **Buy only stocks whose products/services you know and understand.**

Lynch teaches that by using the company's products, you likely know more than the average analyst.

2. **Earnings must grow at a 25 to 50% rate. Avoid above 50% growth.**

Growth above 50% is too high to sustain. However, growth needs to be a minimum of 25% to qualify as a high growth name.

3. **Check the PEG ratio against the average for the sector.**

4. **Inventories must stay equal with sales.**

Excess inventory is a sign of potential trouble ahead. Stockpiling inventory is not a good signal for the company to send.

5. **Strong cash position relative to debt.**

Cash is king, and this is especially so for corporations

6. **Invest for the long term.**

Ignore short-term fluctuations in the market

7. **Don't sell even after 100% returns. Wait for ten-baggers or ten times your investment.**

Don't take profits too soon. Only way to get a ten-bagger is to be patient.

Chapter 21

The Bottom Line, Stay Flexible!

Many investors get hung up on whether they are growth or value investors. Being forced to pick a category of investment philosophy and stick with it is often an exercise in futility. All investors, whether they invest in growing stocks or deep value stocks have the same goal. That goal is portfolio growth regardless of philosophical camp.

Let's take a closer look at growth and value.

One of the most controversial things Warren Buffett is noted for saying is that growth and value stocks are joined at the hip. In other words, there isn't much of a difference between growth and value when it comes to categorizing stocks. While he is correct, there is a difference in the way growth and value investors go about choosing what growing stocks for investment.

The difference lays in the criteria used by both value and growth investors as stock pickers.

Value investors look for stocks whose share price is undervalued when compared to the intrinsic value of the company. In other words, they look for stocks that have been temporarily beaten down in the anticipation of their price rising sometime after their purchase. Apparently this makes sense.

Growth investors often take the opposite tack by purchasing stocks that are often climbing in price. By doing this, growth investors are anticipating that the growing stock will keep on its upward price trajectory. Growth investors believe that the organic nature of the company will continue to attract buyers to the growing stock, hence push the price higher. This philosophy also makes sense.

Not being stuck in any single theory is the lesson I take from Buffett's words. We all have the same goal of buying growing stocks and creating profits. Sometimes the value investing mantra makes sense, other times, it is best to look at the growth investing idea.

Being open to finding both types of opportunities will maximize your profit potential.

Chapter 22

The Value Of News

The worse a situation becomes the less it takes to turn it around, the bigger the upside.
—George Soros

Financial news has substantial influence over the short term nature of price moves.

I have discovered that it is not the severity of the news that has the most effect on price, but rather the novelty of the news.

Take global terrorist attacks, as an example. The first attack, after a period of peace, often shocks stock prices into a sell off. However, subsequent attacks, despite the severity, have less and less of an effect.

As you know, predicting novel news events is an impossibility.

The most effective way to trade such events is to fade the move. One of the most profitable methods, I have ever used, is to wait for a novel market rocking or black swan type event to send the stock market into a tailspin, then go long the major equity indexes like the DJIA or S&P 500. Using ETF's or e-mini future contracts make sense for this style of trading.

The recent BREXIT sell off was a prime example of this strategy working in a huge way. This move made the year for those with the knowledge to use it as a buying opportunity.

GRAB

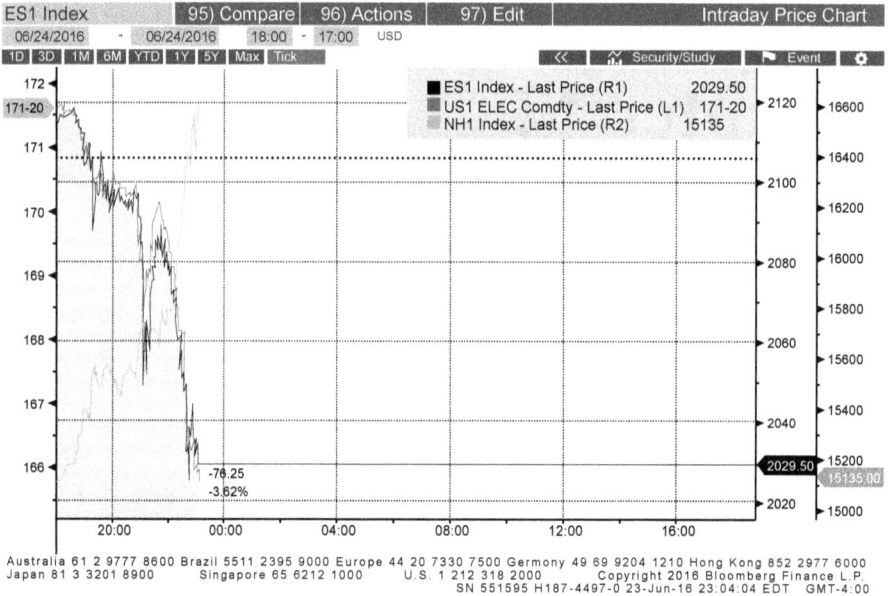

As you know, stocks quickly rallied to new highs after the BREXIT sell off. Those with the knowledge and skill to enter long after such a sell off made a killing.

Having the patience to wait for true black swan novel news events is a highly effective strategy!

Chapter 23

The Truth About Internet Forums

My life was changed by internet trading forums. Among countless benefits, I was able to leveraged my contacts to launch a hedge fund, promote my writing hobby, and to top it off, meet my wife! There is tremendous value gained by participating in such forums. However, it is critical to understand that many financial dangers lurk along with the benefits. This chapter will identify the dangers so that you can avoid them while reaping the benefits!

From the serious discussions on nuclearphynance.com and Willmott.com to Wall Street's popular message board, elitetrader.com there exists distinct categories of posters.

Many traders use these sites for stock tips and picks, market wisdom, getting the latest scoop, news, and even simple entertainment and humor.

Whether you are a weathered skipper of these financial forums or a brand new investor who will look for the first time as soon as you finish this section, it's smart to understand the major categories of participants who provide the information both good and bad, nonsense or invaluable.

Charlatans And Cranks

Understanding the difference between Charlatans and Cranks allows one to quickly categorize the differing voices on message boards.

Simply put, a Crank is a well-meaning nutcase. Cranks truly believe they are helping others with their strange interpretation of the world and markets.

On the other hand, Charlatans know that what they are preaching is wrong yet they continue to do so for monetary gain. Charlatans have an alternative motive for pushing their agenda and know it.

Here's how Cranks and Charlatans fit into the world of financial chat rooms.

First, these sites are chock full of free information but it's important to know how to separate the wheat from the chaff.

The most harmless posters are those who I call the bulls or bears depending on their investment at the time. These normally nice and friendly posters are simply talking their book. For example, if they are long a particular stock they will post glowing reviews, bullish technical analysis charts, positive news stories and/or anything to get you on their side and hopefully jump on board with them helping to push the stock higher. Of course, the opposite would be the bear who will post whatever they feel is needed to deflate the stock price. Some true, some not true. While the bull and bear type can make entertaining reading, it's important to always keep in mind that they are generally only pushing their agenda. Some can have amazing information and tactics that can truly help you in your trading. Others may not even be as knowledgeable as you, so it's critical to read carefully to discern the worthwhile bulls/bears from the merely entertaining.

The second and more insidious denizen of these forums is the internet troll. Troll types exist all over the internet in chat rooms, forums and basically anywhere they can disrupt a legitimate conversation. This creature is definitely not only limited to finance forums but financial sites seem to have more than their fair share. The troll can be easily recognized as someone who will insert inflammatory and generally nonsensical arguments within a normal written conversation.

Some of these trolls will even contradict themselves from topic to topic in an effort to stir things up and cause chaos among the legitimate site users. They are normally users with high post counts who provide very little actual information in their contributions. Trolls will post disparaging and often downright nasty comments in multiple threads for the simple purpose of upsetting other users. A few hours spent perusing various financial sites will reveal multiple troll like personalities. Ignoring and not engaging these chaos lovers is the best course of action.

The third broad category of poster is the finance ghoul. **Ghouls are the Cranks of finance forums.**

Ghouls can be intelligent sounding and are difficult to identify without much experience on a particular site.

Look for strange or difficult to understand verbiage, often within scientific sounding prose. Most Ghouls are simply misled souls who really mean no harm, but can lead you down the rabbit hole of misinformation.

Others seem to genuinely like to confuse and obfuscate simple issues in an effort to appear superior since they understand the topic and you do not. The dangerous thing about ghouls is they can appear to know what they are talking about while it is actually simple nonsense. While reading or posting on a finance forum, keep alert for anyone who seems to answer your questions or contributes with pseudo academic or scientific words that really make no sense when taken in context. You may be dealing with a ghoul.

Finally, the most dangerous type of poster is the stealth vendor. These seemingly harmless contributors often have huge following of new and even seasoned investors. They first come across as wanting to help you become a better investor. However, their true agenda is far different. **Stealth vendors are the Charlatans of internet finance forums.**

Using everyday language, stealth vendors often make outrageous claims to create a following. I have witnessed ridiculous statements like the ability to capture three times the daily range of a future contract and having 98% accuracy rates from stealth vendors.

Stealth vendors are easily identified as being overly helpful and making things seem very simple. Also, they often make grandiose claims about themselves and success rates. Folks that use multiple degree designations after their names in marketing materials, a practice that is considered highly gauche among real academics, is another tip off that the person is a stealth vendor.

If you question or challenge stealth vendors about their claims, they may become very malicious and threatening. I have been threatened with legal action and even physical harm for exposing stealth vendors in the past. Even if the stealth vendor does not threaten you for asking logical questions, the poor, broken souls who follow these types will relentless flame you in an effort to gain points with their guru. It is truly a sad situation learning to quickly recognize and categorize the various internet posters is the first step to maximizing the value of message boards.

Chapter 24

Interviews With Legendary Traders

Swan diving off the tongues of crippled giants
—Neil Faloon

My start in the hedge fund business came from a very unusual source. Tradingmarkets.com, a content provider for Yahoo Finance, assigned me to conduct a series of interviews with leading hedge fund managers, traders, economists, and other financial luminaries.

It was via this assignment that I was able to interact with the best of the best in the financial world. These relationships provided me a solid start in the hedge fund business. I started with a 5th Ave New York City based hedge fund. It was at this fund that I learned the fund business from the ground up from a former Israel Englander's Millennium global macro trader.

Previous to this, I was honored to be accepted into Victor Niederhoffer's inner circle and spent much time at his Connecticut compound. It was here where I learned the critical importance of not taking anything for granted and testing every market claim completely.

These interviews were conducted in 2005. Much has changed in the markets since those days. However, there remains much wisdom in the words of the following legendary traders.

1. Victor Niederhoffer

Victor has become a dear friend of my family and I. His generosity and teaching ability is unparalleled in the world of financial gurus. He is often wrongly maligned due to his several fund implosions despite his numerous achievements and contributions to the financial world.

I'll never forget the first time I was invited to his Connecticut compound. Having followed his career, I knew a little about what to expect, but witnessing him trade in person was truly eye opening.

Victor works and lives on a 13 acre spread with a full-blown trading room above the garage in his mansion. There is a sign outside the trading room wryly stating "Remove Your Shoes Before Entering The Temple". Inside the trading room, there is complete silence and no air conditioning. It is much more like a scientific lab than a traditional trading room. His dozen or so researchers and traders sit to the right and do not speak during the trading day. All communication is done via email and instant messages. Victor's trading station is on the far left with painting of his former boss, George Soros and whaling ships near his desk. Vic is constantly asking his team to test ideas while actively trading. The energy in the room is unbelievably intense yet its near impossible to tell if they are making or losing money on the day.

The following is an interview I conducted to drill into his market philosophy.

Victor is a legendary speculator, market philosopher, gamesman, and racquet sport champion. He worked directly with George Soros and was ranked the number one hedge fund manager in the world for several years then disaster struck. In 1997, an overly expansive speculation in the Thai stock market caused spectacular losses in his accounts. Due to extensive leverage, his losses were magnified over and above his 50% loss in Thailand, and spillover effects from that debacle caused his fund to be well over its head in U.S. equities when they closed down limit on Oct/ 27/1997.

In short, a combined sequence of events – huge declines in individual Thai stocks, losses in the Thai currency and the closing of the U.S. stock market and extensive up moves in the prices of options the fund was short; all came together in one day, in a short and disastrous coincidence. The loss, over and above profits made and withdrawals from the fund, totaled approximately $50 million. In addition to the losses in the funds, Victor had invested heavily in his own trading. To cover his debts and living expenses, after much soul-searching, he took out a mortgage on his house at an interest rate of 18% a year and sold his liquid assets, including his entire silver collection and his holdings in private and publicly held companies. He started again from the bottom. He scraped together a small trading stake and started plying his trade, slowly building back what was lost, determined never ever to allow the same mistake to happen twice. In a true example of the human spirit and his will to be a champion again, he is back in the game at a top level.

Since inception in February 2002, Vic's current fund, "Matador," had a three-year annualized return of 31%, placing it among the top five offshore funds. In 2004, Matador had a 50% return, the best of all offshore funds with more than $45 million in assets, according to the TASS rankings. Here's a gentleman who came from materially meager beginnings, rose to the top academically, athletically, and financially--- lost it all, and is now back on top. He is truly someone we can all learn valuable market and life lessons from, since he has been and succeeded on the front lines in all capacities and levels.

Most investors and traders don't realize the extent of the subterfuge, con games and outright deceit that occur daily in the financial markets. Victor and Laurel have extensively studied, researched and tested the commonly held beliefs of market participants. As described in their recent book "Practical Speculation," they have discovered that many of these beliefs simply do not stand up to rigorous testing and are merely delusions that result in losses. In this interview, we will examine the biggest market con games and how you can profit from these popular delusions.

Dave: Welcome, Victor and Laurel

Victor: Thank you for having us.

Dave: Let's start off by talking about what first perked your interest in "stock market cons".

Victor: Laurel and I have been working together on the philosophy of markets over the last 8 years. The ideas I will present are our joint work and some of them are touched on in our book, "Practical Speculation". Laurel, would you please enlighten Dave as to the genesis of our research into the "Invasion of the Body Snatchers" concept.

Dave: Invasion of the body snatchers! Isn't that a sci-fi movie from the 1950's?

Laurel: Yes, It's a Jack Finney film from 1954. We believe it's the perfect allegory for an introduction to the big market con. The film is about invaders from outer space that take over people's bodies, making them hopeless and listless, ready to accept whatever propaganda they hear. It's a perfect analogy of how investors are misled by market cons

Dave: I see. You believe that the public has been duped by the market's propaganda machine, so to speak?

Victor: Part of the backdrop to our research was the concern about financial reporting and the corruption of corporate executives, as well as the normal issues with the economy like interest rates and international affairs. But there is always something wrong with the backdrop of the market, the economy and individual companies. The problem is, the public is generally mistaken in its enthusiasm for determining whether factors are bullish or bearish

Dave: Are you saying that it's impossible to tell how the market will interpret various factors as positive or negative?

Victor: Yes. Retrospectively, after the market has gone down, it's generally assumed that we are in a bear market and conditions are terrible. This causes the public to lose hope and refuse to take on risk.

Dave: Do bear markets even exist?

Victor: Bear markets only exist in retrospect. This is one of the greatest fallacies in the market. One of the main philosophical points in our book is that it's guaranteed to happen.

Dave: What's guaranteed to happen?

Victor: The public must always believe absolutely, with the strongest conviction, the idea that will make them contribute the most to the market and one of the things the public has to do is sell low and buy high.

Dave: That makes sense. It's how the market feeds and supports itself.

Victor: I wrote about this extensively in my first book, "Education of a Speculator." The dead weight costs of the market are tremendous. In terms of ecology, there's a huge loss of energy in the market. This loss of energy, in market terms, is commissions, communication costs, salaries, fancy offices, etc. These things need to be paid for the market to continue. The public pays these costs, the same way the sun provides the energy for the earth.

Dave: The public needing to buy the tops and sell the bottoms plays right into your aversion to the "trend following" concept of trading. You actually have it listed as number 3 in your 10 big cons of the market. Why?

Victor: I have an aversion to all fixed systems and purportedly easy ways of making money in the market because the market learns and adapts to allow flexible, sagacious and strong decision makers to profit at the expense of the weak.

Dave: OK, why "trend following" in particular?

Victor: The public needs to be tricked or deceived out of their basic role of buy and hold. If they follow the buy and hold mantra, they are going to achieve the Dimsonesque [editors note: Elroy Dimson, Paul Marsh and Mike Staunton co-authored "Triumph of the Optimists" a 2002 book that documented for the first time the 100-year returns of the world's stock markets] returns of 10, 000 fold per century. I am particularly averse to trend following methods because of the following reasons: 1. They are often untested. 2. If tested, their variability is too high to rule out randomness, and 3. If tested relative to uncertainty, they assume past seemingly non-random movements of prices are predictive of what's going to happen in the future.

Dave: Is this strictly for the stock market or all financial markets?

Victor: When trend following methods are tested on the stock market indexes, they tend to show that the correlation of past returns and future returns is negative, and that the number of runs of price changes in the same direction is less than would be expected by chance. I have never seen an example of a real life movement in prices that would allow trend following to work retrospectively, that does not also show positive serial correlations, and an observed number of runs in the same direction that is greater than would have been expected by chance.

Dave: Are you able to support this view with actual numbers?

Victor: In my book "Education of a Speculator," I report that the correlation between weekly stock price changes in the S&P futures during the 1990's is approximately -0.08. The correlation between daily changes is approximately -0.04 over almost all relevant periods. The chances of a rise following a series of 2, 3, 4 or more consecutive declines, in stocks, is approximately 10% higher than normal. Therefore, trend followers in the stock market averages would appear to be playing in a game heavily stacked against them.

Dave: What about the other markets? Do the same studies hold true?

Victor: No. I hasten to add that such tests would not show similar biases against trend following in other markets such as fixed income, or foreign exchange.

Dave: Then what is your objection to trend following in these markets?

Victor: In general, it's the philosophical objection that the followers of long term trends don't take into account one of the fundamental rules of economics, which is that incentives matter.

Dave: Please explain what you mean.

Victor: The supply curve moves outward and to the right when prices rise, and inward to the left when prices decline. Moreover, trend following does not take into account the fundamental tendency of the market to abhor upsetting the apple cart by moving prices to permanent new level, thereby creating threats to its tried and true tendency to make the public lose more than they have any right to, by constantly buying too high and selling too low. If the public were all trend followers, and the vast majority of them are, then prices would be constantly moving to permanently higher or lower levels, and this would be bad for the well-heeled upholders of the market infrastructure who must survive for markets to continue.

Dave: This all seems to make sense in theory. However, how do you explain the fantastic track records of the major trend followers reported in books on the subject or the economic argument that speculators on big moves are paid an economic return by hedgers and equilibrators?

Victor: Well, I would look as a criterion at the total profits that all trend followers have made over time for their public clients rather than the personal profits they have made for themselves. I would also compare the past high returns that the publicly cited great exponents have made to the total dollar amount that their clients have made or lost. In addition, I would look at the actual total dollar returns to the public of those who invested in some of the greatest trend following funds who admittedly have had much inferior results, lawsuits, and tragedies in their publicly reported and audited results versus the legendary stories of great past performance. Another thing I would like to point out is the publicly reported results of the famous trend followers in the last two years, when money at their disposal is at the maximum. I dare say that billions upon billions have been lost, as a review of the rankings of CTA's would show. But of course, that's guaranteed to happen. Looking at the April TASS Flash report, I would estimate the average trend fund is down 20-40% over the last 2 years, and some are really getting killed. Please bear in mind that the big CTA's typically offer 8 or 10 different "programs," so that they can quietly close down the worst performers, or just stop reporting their result.

Dave: Wow, that's some indictment of trend following. Is there anything else on this subject?

Victor: Of course, I am just getting started! I normally don't like to talk about this subject since it foments much hatred against me. Many of the proponents of trend following are attempting to market systems, seminars and funds based upon the concept, and I stand as a reasoned voice against their profits and thus must be discredited for their own survival. With that said, my major objection to trend following is that it doesn't take into account one of the most important regularity of the markets, aside from the laws of incentive, and the immense degree of deception and big cons---i.e. the principle of ever-changing cycles . The public is always behind the form. I would even go so far to compare the concept of trend following to a cult like scientology. It's impossible to have a rational discussion with some of its proponents since so many people have vested interest in perpetuating the myth.

Dave: We are on a roll on this subject, let me see if I can dig a little deeper into your thoughts on the concept of market trends. Do you believe that trends don't exist at all or simply that an existing trend is not tradable?

Victor: Any trend that exists can be quantified and its departure from randomness can be measured with the usual statistical procedures, such as confidence intervals and likelihoods. Serial correlation coefficients, regression coefficients of current changes versus past changes, and magnitudes of the impact of past moving averages on the future, distributions of the length of runs, the correllelogram, the expected waiting times between peaks and valleys, survival statistics. All these techniques are very good at discovering any non-random elements.

To join a proper debate, such measures must be quantified for various markets and various times, and the degree of uncertainty and departure from randomness must be ascertained. I have never found a movement in prices that anyone could make money with by a trend following method that didn't also show a major departure from randomness revealed by the standard statistical measures I mentioned. The tragedy is the mysticism and blind acceptance of trendism, that trend following exponents proclaim, without any evidence as to magnitude and uncertainty. No self-reported results that selected individuals or leaders might have made in the past shed light on the debate.

Dave: Your well-known saying, "If it can be tested, it must be tested" comes into play here. Exactly what testing have you done to prove the above idea?

Victor: These tests can readily be performed my group of colleagues performs these tests maybe 2-3 thousand times a year over different markets and time frames. Those of a cognitive bent and those with their feet on the ground are always open to the existence of trends, but they test them with the best statistical methods existing. If you apply these tests to stock market moves, you will find that all such tests show negative serial correlation. In fact, they indicate a tendency for reversal.

Dave: What about the upward bias in stock prices? Why can't that be interpreted as a trend?

Victor: Well, all proper statistical tests take into account this upward drift. They would look for serial correlations over and above the basic drift of the market. One of the other market cons is the permanent bearishness of some of market pundits, and I am the last person to say that this upward drift, evidenced over the last 200 years, does not exist. This in no way refutes, but it does refine the statistical tests required for the stock market. However, I hasten to add that no such upward drift exists in any other market.

Dave: Very insightful, Victor. Your last sentence opens up the next big market con—commodities are better for the long term than stocks. Can you elaborate on this topic?

Victor: This con is very closely related to the trend following big con. There is no upward drift in commodities.

Dave: That idea really flies in the face of the recent increased interest in commodities as promoted by a certain world traveling commodity fund manager.

Victor: Yes, I believe you interviewed him recently. This type of renewed public interest seems to be indicating a top soon. The fact that money was made in the past buying commodities in no way indicates that this will continue. The Niederhoffer/Kenner camp believes in the principle of ever changing cycles. It's one of our hallmarks.

Dave: Wait a second, Victor. Ever changing cycles? That sounds like a contradiction to me. If a cycle is ever changing, it's no longer a cycle. What am I missing?

Victor: That's an excellent question, Dave. The idea of ever changing cycles comes from a racetrack bettor whose insights and value to the public are far superior to even the greatest stock market experts. His name was Robert Bacon, and he wrote a book called "Secrets of Professional Turf Betting."

Laurel: Bacon also called the concept the principle of ever-changing trend. His great insight was that even if the public ever managed to overcome the crazy urge to gamble and got wise to a winning idea, the principle of ever-changing trends would quickly and drastically change the results. As he wrote, "The would-be professional player must always understand that the form moves away from the public's knowledge."

Victor: Unfortunately, the book is out of print and has become very difficult to buy. We also recommend "Horse Trading" by Ben Green, and that is much easier to obtain.

Laurel: We've posted some excerpts from Bacon on our Web site, www.dailyspeculations.com. He explains ever-changing trends this way: Say an owner who had been sending his star racehorse out to do its best at odds of 3-to-1 cooled off as the prices sank below 5-to-2. He tells the jockey to win if he can win easily, but to pull back out of the money in the stretch if he sees that an easy winning was not possible. That way, the bad race will put the public off the horse for next time.

Dave: Horse racing and trading, Victor, Laurel? Isn't that stretching things a bit?

Victor: Not at all, the concepts are very similar. There are two things that happen—the payoff goes down if the horse wins, and the payoff reduction is such that even if the horse were to win with the same probability the system becomes unprofitable. The horse racing business is very similar to the stock market in this way. Strangely enough, most of the major horseracing systems of the 1930's have the same philosophical underpinnings as trend following systems. They basically say take the horse that's winning the most, bet on him, and stay away from the horse that's losing the most. The horse racing people actually have a much higher standard of analysis than the proponents of the current stock market systems. The horse bettors always demand workouts, unlike many practitioners of the trend following systems.

Dave: Let me see if I understand how the horse betting systems relates to trend following. Everyone bets on the horse that is in a winning trend, thereby reducing the payoff should that horse win again?

Victor: Correct, but, Bacon says that would be true if the percentage of wins were the same and here's his fantastic insight: the percentage of wins does not stay the same; it goes down because the owners like to bet on their own horses. Therefore, if the odds are 2 to 1 for a win, they don't bet as much or push the horse as much as they would when the odds are 10 to one. The chances of winning is actually greater the fewer wins a horse has.

Dave: I see how that would relate to trend following systems.

Victor: Those systems are designed to create the same situation on paper. These systems look good in the past, and they look good with small amounts of money—10, 20, 50 million dollars -- thereby luring the public to put billions and billions into it. Then they fail. There are people who must exist for the markets to survive; these are the easy money people. It's the big players who see the exponents of easy money coming. The people who are flexible, analytical and scientific—like those who read our books and those who read your interviews trying to find the insights—are the ones who survive and thrive in the market.

Dave: Thanks for the compliment to my readers! So, you are saying that flexibility is the key to success in the market?

Victor: That's one key. One needs to have strength, flexibility and a foundation. People should know this intuitively. Most people understand this via playing cards or any sport for that matter. It is a fact that deception is rampant and flexibility wins the game. Those people who play the same game and are predictable are easy prey. This is another reason why even in those markets that test well for trend following, we have an aversion to accept it as a given. This all relates back to the fact that the anecdotal method does not prove anything. This "My dad can beat up your dad" nonsense is a real waste of time. Many CTA's and hedge fund managers become very wealthy, but this does not prove that they have made money for the public. It means they make a lot on fees.

Dave: Let's move on to the next big con, the fund of funds. It seems to make sense to me that diversifying a fund into multiple funds would be a good thing. Why is this concept a con?

Victor: I like to say that all funds of funds will converge to a Sharpe ratio of minus 1000.

Dave: What?

Victor: Well, that is just a figure of speech. Actually, the issue is the fees. They pay fees on about 10 different levels, but that is not the worst of it. Currently, most of these funds tend to be equally weighted on the long and short side. Therefore, since the market is pretty much a random walk with a positive drift of 10% or so a year, they end up with a zero percent return. They make 10% on their longs, lose 10% on their shorts, and often pay multiple fees. It's a losing proposition for everyone but the manager.

Dave: Moving onto another one of your favorite big market cons, technical analysis. Many traders trade exclusively with TA. Why do you consider it a con?

Victor: Everything is part of the basic philosophical backdrop that we discussed earlier. TA tends to unleash people from the fundamental foundation that they need to be successful.

Dave: It gives most traders false hope. Is that what you are saying?

Victor: That is part of it. It also gets traders to trade too quickly. It makes people fearful and elated, causing too much turnover -- and turn over is very expensive in this game.

Dave: Do you see any value at all to technical analysis?

Victor: Many of my best friends are technical analysts and I am actually a technical analyst myself. However, the kind of technical analysis I perform is scientific. I put forth hypothesis, I test them, I consider the uncertainty, I quantify them, I try to put them in an economic framework. When done in this manner, TA has value. What I don't believe in is the idea that the visual intuiting of price charts can give much insight into the subsequent distribution of prices. This is the way most people view TA and why TA cons most traders. I do believe that the interplay of markets, and price distributions, are of a highly predictive nature.

Dave: These predictive distributions and market interplay is how you make decisions in the market?

Victor: It's what I am most renowned for. A large part of the managed account industry in one way or another started out with this basic idea that I pioneered. Monroe Trout, Roy Niederhoffer and Toby Crabel, among many others started at my firm. A number of managers with over a billion dollars under management started with me. This makes it much harder for me since many of my former top people are using and augmenting my methods elsewhere, and of course, my ideas become subject to the principle of ever-changing trends.

Dave: Correct me if I am wrong, Victor. But, I think your studies have shown some value in the VIX indicator. Is this accurate?

Victor: That is an example of a fixed system, a shooting star. In general, a good rule of thumb is when the market is looking terrible that's a very good time to buy and when it's looking great it's a good time to reduce your exposure. Not to short it -- I don't ever believe in selling the stock market short. The VIX is very highly correlated with the recent market move, so it's very hard to separate the VIX from the current market move. A very good predictor of future VIX is the current VIX.

Dave: Explain what you mean by this, please.

Victor: If the VIX is 14% now the best predictor of where it will be in a year is 14%. There is nothing "too high" or "too low" about it. There are just as many factors that will pull it down as will pull it up. There are many statistical measures to forecast volatility. The book by F.X. Diebold, "The Elements of Forecasting" is excellent in this regard. Changes in VIX have a much better forecasting ability than the levels themselves.

Dave: You mean the rate of change?

Victor: Yes, if VIX changes in a one-month period by several percentage points, this is the kind of indicator, in conjunction with the market move, that is a proper area for testing.

Dave: Moving back into market cons. One of the heroes of investors is an individual named Benjamin Graham. His "Security Analysis" book is the bible to value investors and required reading in many business programs. What was his actual performance in the market?

Victor: Abysmal! His performance in romance was much superior to his performance in the market. The Rea-Graham fund applied Ben's ideas over a 15-year period, and it was one of the worst performing mutual funds of all time. He actually got out of the market when the Dow was 500, believing there was no way it could go very much higher. However, that's anecdotal evidence. He could have very good insights even if his performance as an investor was poor. The fact is his book is very shoddy, not scientific. I consider his basic idea of value investing one of the worst big cons.

Dave: Value investing is a con! Why?

Victor: In general, you get paid for taking risk in the market. The basic idea of value investing is to invest in companies that can't lose money. If you can't lose money there's no profit, there's no return, since there is an unchanging demand structure. The rate of return quickly goes down to the risk-free rate.

Dave: Isn't the Sage of Omaha the best-known value investor?

Victor: Yes, he used to invest in things like farm equipment, candy stores, shoe manufacturing, textile plants with tax losses. These are the kinds of companies where the rate of return is usually less than the risk-free rate. Practically speaking, I happen to know something about valuing companies. I ran the largest merger business involved with selling private companies to public companies. I visited thousands of companies. My people sold over 1500 companies. One can never sell one of these value companies above its liquidating value. If you could, there would be tremendous competition to drive it down. That's the economic argument. The real-world argument is that the kind of companies the Sage boasts about buying in 5 minutes are simply not the stocks you want to buy.

Dave: OK, growth is where the average investor should be, and avoid value stocks?

Victor: Yes. The one study that I consider superior to all others is the Value Line study. They set out to prove that value is where to be, but the study proved that growth has beat value by about 20 to 1. It's a real-life study unlike many others.

Dave: Wow that sure is impressive. Is this why you don't buy stocks with a low P/E?

Victor: Yes. Low P/E stocks tend to be the "value" stocks that have a rate of return close to the risk-free rate. The average IPO is priced by the underwriters to yield 50-60% per year. This is in normal times. When people are so risk-averse, as they have been for the last few years, the underwriters discount the yield to make the IPO more appealing.

Dave: Laurel, I would like to direct this next question to you. In "Practical Speculation," you talk about an indicator that I find fascinating, it seems counter-intuitive like many of the things you and Victor have discovered,—you call it the stadium indicator. Tell me a little about what happens to a company after they sign a stadium naming deal?

Laurel: This question needs to put into the general framework of culture. The consequences of the hubris, excess and expansive behavior Hubris was a favorite theme of the ancient Greek historians and storytellers, who used it to show the fate in store for the arrogant and the boastful. The stories are still highly relevant today. The stadium indicator was a number of hubris indicators we invented and tested for "Practical Speculation". We looked at CEOs who said, "We're No. 1," and at companies that announced they would be building the world's highest skyscraper as headquarters, and at companies who named stadiums after themselves.

There were plenty of anecdotes that saw their stock prices plunge after they named stadiums after themselves. Enron's pre-bankruptcy $100 million stadium deal comes to mind, and 3Com and CMGI saw their stock prices fall from the clouds. To find whether there was any general truth to the idea, we did a systematic study. We found that stocks performed significantly worse than the S&P 500 after acquiring stadium naming rights, both that year and the subsequent year.

Victor: What we have found is that the companies that tend to be most hubristic tend to be the ones that perform the worst.

Dave: Pride goeth before a fall.

Victor: Exactly. Related to this is our baseball indicator.

Laurel: This one goes back to what we were saying about expansiveness and excess in popular culture. We found that when home run hitting records are being broken right and left, a down market tends to follow. Think Babe Ruth in the 1920s. When the rules of the game change to favor pitchers over hitters, and teams start focusing more on defense—hitting singles and stealing bases—that seems to portend an up market.

Victor: These indicators are cultural examples of how excesses cause the public to be betting on the wrong type of horse at the wrong time.

Dave: I can see how all these factors you mentioned tie together. Now let's get down to the nitty gritty. How do you trade?

Victor: I am happy you see the correlations. What we teach in our book is to try to understand the forces involved the market. Pay attention to rates on fixed income versus the rates of return on the stock market. Pay attention to buybacks as signals, cash earnings versus accrual accounting, negative serial correlations in stock market indexes. But of course, our book was a worst-seller. They didn't even have a copy of it in my local bookstore. We are happy there are a few eagles out there who gave us a good review. "Active Trader" magazine and the "Journal of Investment Management" are two.

Dave: We are almost out of time. Is there anything you would like to leave our readers with?

Victor: I try to teach a method of thinking. We are dedicated to try to deflate ballyhoo and create a proper framework for proper stock market decision-making.

Dave: Victor, Laurel—Thank you for joining me today. I truly appreciate your time.

Victor: It was our pleasure. Thank you.

2. Jim Rogers

This was one of the stranger interviews I conducted. Jim was nothing but cordial and accommodating but he insisted on running on a treadmill while I was questioning him! We conducted the interview while he was living in his New York City brownstone but has since moved to China due to the incredible opportunities there.

Jim started with humble beginnings and became one of the top money managers of all time. He is an inspiration to people the world over who yearn for adventure and celebrate the human spirit.

This interview will start out by providing Jim's background, his basic investing philosophy and then delve deeper into his mind via our conversation.

It is important to note that he stressed that he is not a trader, but rather believes in waiting patiently until the perfect time to buy or sell appears.

He states that most people need to be playing all the time; this is their downfall according to him. He also believes that his flexibility to buy anything around the worlds the other key to success.

Jim started in the markets in 1968 with just $600.00.

In 1973, he was fortunate enough to meet George Soros with whom he started the Quantum Fund. Jim was the analyst at the fund with George being the trader.

This partnership proved to be a super success with gains approaching 4000% while the SP 500 gained a measly 50%. Jim was able to retire at age 37 to follow his passion for adventure and investments. His first worldwide adventure involved riding a BMW motorcycle 100,000 miles across 6 continents. This trip is chronicled in the book Investment Biker.

In 1999, he began the Millennium Adventure where he and his finance, Paige (now wife) traveled around the world in a custom-built Mercedes convertible. Jim documented every stage of this journey on his website www.jimrogers.com and book Adventure Capitalist.

His passion for investing has led to the creation of The Rogers International Commodities Index and matching fund.

At the time of the interview, the fund has had the best performance record of any fund, regardless of class, over the previous several years with returns approaching 170 %.

His latest book Hot Commodities focuses on the coming monster bull market in commodities.

He believes that the time is perfect to go long the commodities we use daily. Things like sugar, cotton, corn and oil are poised to follow thru or begin a bull market that should last for the next 10-20 years. Let's get started with the interview!

I am privileged to be joined today with Jim Rogers, commodity trader and world adventurer. How are you today Jim?

Jim: Doing just fine.

Dave: First I want to start by getting a little of your history. I know you started at five years old selling peanuts.

Jim: I did in fact. I grew up in a small town in Alabama. There wasn't much money there, so we all started working pretty early. I worked for a concession in the small town.

Later I got the concession, sold peanuts and soft drinks. That was my first venture.

Dave: Talk about humble beginnings. I know you went to Yale, and then joined up with George Soros.

Jim: Yes, I went to Yale, was in the army, and then met George Soros in 1970.

Dave: That is a stroke of luck, how did you manage to meet Mr. Soros?

Jim: I don't recall. I believe someone introduced us. I think he was looking for someone to work with him and I was looking for a job, so it worked.

Dave: You have a new book out called Hot Commodities, what is the basic premise of the book?

Jim: Well, people do not know much about commodities and they think they are unclean. The book is an attempt to explain commodities to people. I try to explain that commodities are an easy way to invest and a safe way to invest if you do your homework. You will also make more money in commodities than you will in stocks and bonds. If I am correct, we are in one of many periodic bull markets in commodities and it is going to last another ten to twenty years and people should be aware of it. Most people who don't know about commodities run for the hills when you talk about commodities.

Dave: For a stock trader, someone who doesn't know anything about commodities but knows about stocks, are there any similarities between the two?

Jim: Well, just because someone has heard of a stock, or has bought a stock does not mean they know what they are doing. Commodities are much simpler than stocks. Let's take copper for instance. When there is too much copper it's going to go down, when there is not enough copper it's going to go up. It's very simple. When you are going to buy a stock, you have to worry about management, the stock market, the government, environmentalists, unions, regulations, world affairs, and 100 other things. Copper is really simple, its either going to go up or down. If copper goes up, copper stocks might not go up because of all the other things I mentioned which can cause complication. So in short, commodities are a lot simpler than stocks.

Dave: Looking at your Rogers International Commodities Index and I noticed that oil has the heaviest weighting at 35%. Why?

Jim: Well, if you look around you oil is the most important commodity in the world. Just looking around the room where you are, there probably isn't a lot of orange juice in that room but there is an abundance of oil. You got to that room by energy. There is electricity. There is a telephone, which came from and runs on energy. The carpet was made from energy. Energy is everywhere and it is the most important commodity in the world.

Dave: Wheat is your second heaviest weighting at 7%. Can you explain this?

Jim: Sure, most people in the world eat some wheat and get some one way or another. Bread comes from wheat for the most part. Wheat and food is very important and in my mind wheat is the single most important commodity traded in the world.

Dave: Do you ever adjust the weighting in your Index fund?

Jim: Well, if we had to yes. I wanted an Index that was transparent, consistent, and stable. I wanted to know what I was investing in. So far, there have been minimal changes. Now if we found out wheat causes cancer, the wheat market would dry up, and it would drop off. If we found out orange juice cures, cancer it would get a larger weight because the volume would skyrocket. If oil became obsolete, of course it will disappear, and we will adjust. Now the Goldman Sachs index has 73% energy right now, but more importantly it changes wildly every year. In my book, I have the annual changes in the Goldman Sachs components and it's just wild. If we are talking about my money, I want to know what I am investing in. In the Goldman Sachs index you don't have a clue what you will be investing in next year, and worse if it goes up Goldman Sachs buys more of it. That is not the way most investors work.

Dave: How much capital do you have in your fund right now?

Jim: Several hundred million dollars.

Dave: What is the minimum for an investor?

Jim: For a retail investor its $10,000. For a qualified investor its $500,000 with lower fees and lower commissions.

Dave: What have the returns been since the inception of the fund?

Jim: We are up about 170% since 1998. It has outperformed everything in the world, every index in any asset class. It is not because of me, it's because it's an index fund. The point is that commodities are in a bull market and that has-been the place to be, it is the place to be, and it will continue to be the place to be.

Dave: I know a while ago you were pretty bearish on the dollar. Are you still bearish on the dollar?

Jim: Well the dollar has been pounded. I read an article a couple years ago that talked about why the dollar was going to collapse. Anything that goes down that fast that much should rise. So it would not surprise me if it did rally. I am not a trader so it's not a prediction. But if and when it rallies for a few days, weeks, months, or a year or so, I am not sure how it's going to rally, I would sell it because the dollar is in terminal decline.

Dave: Do you see a potential intervention in the dollar? Perhaps the Federal Reserve stepping in and supporting it?

Jim: Well they might try. It would have to be a foreign government because our Federal Bank doesn't have any money so they couldn't support it. Our cash reserves are something like $70 billion, while $2 trillion gets traded every day in the currency market. Our $70 billion would be gone in about six to eight minutes. If someone does intervene they know the dollar is so fundamentally unsound, there isn't much they can do other than a temporary or short-term basis.

Dave: Do you feel the same way about the Euro, or do you feel the Euro is a bit safer?

Jim: Well the Euro is less flawed than the dollar and its fundamentals are much better. I own the Euro but don't expect it to survive 15 years from now. However, it is less flawed then than the dollar.

Dave: Do you use technical analysis at all?

Jim: No, it's pretty simple just figuring out what is going on in the world. I try to find things that are cheap and invest in them if I see some positive change coming. I don't understand the charts. Don't misunderstand me, I do look at the charts, but I only look at a simple long-term chart to see what has happened over the last 15 years or so, not to tell me what is going to happen in the future. For example, if I am looking at sugar, I want to know the high, the low, when, why, and things like that. I look at the charts to educate me, rather than a predicting tool.

Dave: In 2002, you completed the Millennium adventure. Did that trip change your perspective?

Jim: My trip was three years around the world, 116 countries, and 152,000 miles later. Sure, it changed my perspective. It made me want to simplify my life. It made me want to have a child. It changed a lot of things.

Dave: On a lighter note, I know you took an assortment of CDs with you on the trip. Can you tell us a little bit about the music you played on the journey?

Jim: Well the list is on my website. I don't recall the exact names anymore but somewhere Mozart, Beethoven, the Fine Young Cannibals, Willy Nelson, and others.

Dave: Wow, pretty eclectic tastes in music. Getting back on track here, I know you have a strong opinion about the US tax code. Can you fill me in?

Jim: Sure, the US tax code is a disaster. Forget the philosophy behind the code, but the actual code itself. With tens of thousands of pages, nobody has a clue what it says. That includes the IRS and the government. You call up the IRS and ask them a question they will say to you, We will give you our opinion, but you can't hold it us to it. It's because they don't even know what it says. It is a minefield. A disaster of boggling proportions.

Dave: Let's talk about the underlying philosophy of the US Tax Code. Why is it flawed?

Jim: The philosophy behind it is that we discourage savings and investing in this country, and we encourage consumption. If you earn money, you pay taxes on it. Then you put the rest in a bank, and they will make you pay taxes on your interest. If you buy a stock, they make you pay taxes on the dividends. Remember the company has already paid income taxes as well. Then you have to pay taxes on the dividend on the money you have saved and invested. So you are already taxed several times. Then if you have capital gains, you have to pay taxes again. Later in life, you will get social security and pay taxes on that money. Now remember Social Security was designed to take your money away from you and hold it in reserve for when you retire and then they give it back to you. They are giving you back your own money but they are making you pay taxes again. God forbid you should die, because if you do you really pay some taxes. Now this is money you have saved, you have invested; you have paid taxes on five, six, or seven times by now. Other countries don't do it this way. They encourage people to save and invest. They don't tax savings. They don't tax investments. We need to change our tax code dramatically.

Dave: If you were in charge of changing the tax code right now, what would be the first thing that you do?

Jim: I would abolish the income tax. We don't need the IRS and we don't need an income tax. We should have a consumption tax. This would save billions of dollars on bureaucrats, tax lawyers, accountants. We would save hundreds of millions of hours of all of us trying to figure out our taxes. The country would be amazingly more efficient, and we would be discouraging consumption. If you didn't consume you wouldn't pay any taxes. If you saved all your money you wouldn't pay any taxes, so it would encourage people to save.

Dave: Wrapping up, do you have any advice to our members who may be just graduating from college now and want to get into trading, finance or the markets?

Jim: Well my advice would be to take a job in research somewhere where you can spend time maturing and finding out how it all really happens. You may find that you are better at trading, and you don't need any research. However, I would spend some time working for someone as an assistant analyst to learn how it is done. I would also suggest that they get a mentor and not just go in with both feet by themselves. In other words, to work for someone else because even if they are bad, at least you will learn why he is bad, and in turn learn how to be good.

Dave: Well, Jim, we are out of time, it's been an honor speaking with you.

Jim: Thank you, let's do it again sometime.

As an endnote, I gained several basic investing principles from my research and conversation with Jim Rogers. They are:

1. **Be patient**— This is most difficult for traders. Jim believes that one of the keys to success in investing is waiting for the perfect time to strike. The urge to constantly be trading causes many to fail.

2. **Expand your horizons**— Look outside of your comfort zone for opportunities. Don't just be a someone trick pony. If you trade stocks, start looking at commodities and vice versa. Jim travels the world searching for the next market to invest. We can all perform a version of this by keeping our eyes and ears open for any potential opportunity.

3. **Use Fundamentals**—Jim doesn't trade with Technical Analysis and charts. Yes, he looks at charts to see what has happened in the past, but does not use them to project the future. He only invests in things that have strong fundamental reasons to be trending.

4. **Think long-term** —Many investors have too short a time period for their investments to perform. Jim rarely even changes the commodity weightings in his fund, preferring to ride the trend as far as possible. This conviction has resulted in him managing the number one performing fund in the world.

5. **Utilize commonsense**—When I asked Jim why he believes that commodities are going to be the next monster bull market, he responded by saying its common sense. This response threw me off track for a bit until I realized the brilliant simplicity of his statement. He followed up by asking me to look around the room and observe the different objects seeing what they were made of. I saw things made of copper, oil, and wheat among other commodities. Everyone uses commodities in some fashion and they are in limited supply. As Jim would say, common sense.

3. Nelson Freeberg

Today's traders are forced to learn about automation in an effort to beat the machines at their own game. This interview is with one of the best trading system builders on earth.

Nelson is a renowned trading systems designer who counts many world-class systematic money managers as clients, including Paul Tudor Jones. He publishes the popular Formula Research letter that focuses on trading system development and is truly on the cutting edge of this field. This interview will step inside his mind to see what we can learn. Let's get started!

Dave: Welcome, Nelson.

Nelson: Thanks, it's a pleasure!

Dave: Let's start at the beginning. What first got you interested in trading system development?

Nelson: Almost no one in the field of systematic trading started out as a trader. Even some of the best-known names in the profession began in different fields. Gerald Appel was a psychiatric social worker. Martin Zweig was a professor of academic finance. The late Bruce Babcock, who popularized dozens of mechanical timing strategies, was an assistant district attorney (who helped prosecute Charles Manson).

Dave: Wow, that's a shocker. I would have never guessed that is the case. Charlie Manson, the market? More similarities than we would like to admit! *(Laughter all around)*. Seriously, did researchers from these diverse fields reach any common conclusions?

Nelson: When all of these people eventually turned their attention to money management, they reached a common conclusion. Buy-and-hold investing simply does not work. There may be periods when the stock market goes straight up. But the good times are offset by frequent bear markets.

Dave: How do the systematic traders earn more than simple buy-and-hold strategies?

Nelson: One way to capture the gains and avoid the risks is to use conventional technical analysis—familiar tools like charting, candlesticks, trend line analysis, etc. But there is a lot of subjectivity involved in interpreting chart formations, breakouts, volume patterns, and so forth. This puts a lot of negative psychological pressure on the trader. Furthermore, there is no easy way to back test-trading methods that rely on intuition and judgment.

Dave: Correct, technical analysis is generally very subjective, often an art instead of a science.

Nelson: Yes, so the alternative is mechanical timing methods. Explicit trading rules can be reliably tested in great historical depth. If they don't work, all you've lost is time and effort. You don't lose real money. Furthermore, much of the doubt and fear inherent in subjective trading is eliminated when the entry and exit rules are specified in advance and rest on sound principles of price behavior.

Dave: How did you start being interested in systematic trading?

Nelson: I was working on a Ph.D. in world politics at Columbia University in the late 1970s. My specialty was strategic arms control. I would use formulas and models to simulate the effects of thermonuclear war. (Please understand I was trying to REDUCE the odds of such catastrophe.) Around that time, gold and silver were on a historic bull run. My cousin, a professional commodity trader, introduced me to the joys and passion of trading. And I was hooked…just like that.

Dave: You were a scientist, I see. Did you give up on the world politics studies?

Nelson: I quit researching world politics and shifted to the study of price behavior. Like many of us, I had my ups and downs as a chartist. Sometimes the chart patterns worked, other times they didn't. Meanwhile, around this same time, the personal computer made its appearance. It became much easier to develop and test mechanical timing strategies. For ten years, I researched computerized timing methods, trading all along. In 1991, I started Formula Research to share my quantitative findings. We started out with a small but discerning group (including Zweig, Appel and Paul Jones). Today we serve institutional money managers and private investors in 27 countries.

Dave: Let's give systematic trading a clear definition. How *exactly* do you define systematic trading?

Nelson: It's simply rule-based trading. Investment decisions are based on specified entry and exit conditions defined in advance. With a systematic timing model, if we all have access the same price data, we should generate identical signal histories—a feat not possible with trading by judgment.

Dave: What are the basic components of a trading system?

Nelson: As is often (correctly) pointed out, some of the best trading systems are the simplest. You just need an entry rule to get you in the market and an exit rule to get you out.

Dave: Interesting, particularly in light of all the "quant shops" opening up.

Nelson: By the way, all things being equal, simpler is indeed better. But I would not exclude in principle trading strategies which embrace more nuance and are therefore more complex.

Dave: Are all trading systems basically the same?

Nelson: Most trend-following systems are surprisingly similar in their governing logic. They will feature distinctive stops, filters, and other individual variations but over a test period going back decades, the equity curves will track each other closely.

Dave: What about intraday systems?

Nelson: As for S&P day trading systems, my friends at Futures Truth have tested dozens of intraday models. They note that almost all S&P day trading systems incorporate an intraday breakout entry (trend following) as well as a reversal entry (countertrend). In essence, while S&P day trading system vary in detail, many adhere to this same dual structure.

Dave: That similarity can be very broad. Is the inner logic basically the same also?

Nelson: No, that is where the differences lay. I must have several hundred trading systems in my personal library of timing strategies. In terms of the logic and structure of these systems, there is a wealth of diversity.

Dave: Do system entry and exit rules rely on the same logic?

Nelson: Oh yeah. But the entry and exit rules don't have to symmetrical. For instance, one of the best long-term stock market timing strategies ever developed (in this case by the distinguished market analyst Martin Pring) uses asymmetrical entry and exit logic. You buy stocks when the S&P 500 is above its 12-month moving average AND the yield on 90-day commercial paper is below its 12-month smoothing. You sell and exit to the money market when EITHER indicator crosses its 12-month average in the opposite direction.

Dave: When developing a system— is, back testing a viable method to determine its potential success?

Nelson: Back-testing is not just viable, it's indispensable.

Dave: Is there specific criteria that you use to analyze whether a system is successful? In other words, what gains should a system produce in relation to draw downs?

Nelson: Well, the ratio of return to drawdown will vary greatly depending on how much back testing is done. The greater the extent of historical testing, the lower the gain in relation to the drawdown.

Dave: Should all traders use the same evaluation techniques?

Nelson: Most institutional analysts evaluate an investment strategy by looking at its compound annual return and maximum draw down on a percentage basis. If the strategy offers a higher compound annual return than the S&P 500 while limiting maximum drawdown to, say, 15% of equity, that would be a promising start. By contrast, in commodity trading, most analysts look at the gains and draw down on a dollar basis. Here a good benchmark is to limit draw down to under 10-15% of net profit.

Dave: Are most trading systems trend based?

Nelson: Many successful trading systems are exclusively trend following. Others are both counter-trend and trend-sensitive. I would say that most trading systems have a trend-following component.

Dave: How specifically do you determine and define trend?

Nelson: Timing models use many different ways to define a trend: Moving average crossovers, percent swing reversals, channel breakouts including Donchian, Bollinger or Keltner Bands; Wilder's Parabolic and Volatility formulas. Some people even use countertrend indicators like to RSI to identify a trend. For example, you buy when RSI climbs above 50 and sell on a cross below 50.

Dave: Are there inherent flaws that must be dealt with when determining trend?

Nelson: Well, the main weakness of a trend-following strategy is its susceptibility to false signals. With most purely trend-following systems, the percentage of winning trades is 40%-45%.

Dave: Is there a way around the issues with trend-based systems?

Nelson: The only way I know of to reduce whipsaws is to add some external filter. A good example is the Pring stock market strategy I described above. You can only go long stocks when the price trend is bullish and the monetary trend is bullish (as represented by lower commercial paper yields). But when you add such a fundamentally inspired component, it is imperative that your exit be exclusively trend following. Why? Because eventually that monetary filter is going to fail. (See Japan in the 1990s, the U.S. in the 1930s).

Dave: Recently, several of the huge trend funds have been suffering large draw downs. Is this implicit in the system OR is the system probably being managed poorly?

Nelson: I believe strongly that these recurring lapses are inevitable when you bet everything on a strictly trend-following model. Periodic losses come with the territory, no matter how well the investment managers execute their strategy.

Dave: What other aspects, other than trend, can a trading system be based on?

Nelson: You can use counter trend strategies to try to anticipate tops and bottoms. In other words, you rely on indicators like stochastics and RSI to identify overbought and oversold conditions. You can also add fundamental, sentiment, intermarket or other indicators external to the actual price data to supplement and reinforce your ability to capture the trend.

Dave: Getting practical, let's design a basic trading system. First, how much data is needed before we start?

Nelson: In a word, you need a representative data sample, one that incorporates strong trends up, weak trends up, strong trends down, weak trends down, and extended periods of congestion. How much data you need will depend on the time frame and the market. A long-term weekly system for institutional stock investors will require data in greater historical depth than an S&P day trading system that uses 1-minute bars.

Dave: After the data is gathered, what's the first step?

Nelson: You first have to decide whether the system will be general in nature, designed to trade a diverse portfolio of commodities or stocks. Alternatively, you could develop a profitable strategy that only trades one sector, say energy products or stock index futures.

Dave: Let's go over each of those versions.

Nelson: Sure, if you are trading a diverse portfolio of commodities (Option I above), you will probably use a trend-following strategy. You need historical price data and a testing platform that is capable of simulation across a portfolio of markets in dynamic interaction. If your system is designed to trade a single market or sector (Option II above), say the S&P 500 futures, you will need to decide whether you want to add any predictive inputs to complement whatever price-based logic you start out with.

Davao, what's the next step?

Nelson: The next step is build your system using only a restricted sample of the data. Once your method works on this finite segment of price history, you can test it on the out-of-sample data you prudently reserved for confirmation.

Dave: The Monte Carlo simulation model?

Nelson: Yes, exactly.

Dave: Are transaction costs included in the output?

Nelson: Yes, especially in short-term commodity testing.

Dave: What about slippage?

Nelson: Ditto.

Dave: How does an effective system handle slippage and transaction costs?

Nelson: Slippage and commissions become more significant constraints as the time frame is scaled to progressively lower intervals, which increases trading activity. If you have a long-term institutional stock market strategy that trades three times a year, you don't have to worry as much about transaction costs. But if you are developing an intraday trading system for the S&P 500 with 30 entries per day, you will find slippage and commissions to be a major, possibly lethal burden. You must find a way to filter out most of the poor trades.

Dave: Are the above simple system guidelines applicable to most systems?

Nelson: Well, the same general principles apply.

Dave: Wrapping this up, what is the most critical aspect of a trading system?

Nelson: The same as your evaluation of any portfolio manager or investment program. You have to minimize drawdown in relation to investment gains.

Nelson: Well, the key to system building is testing, re-testing and more testing.

Dave: Thank you for your time today!

Nelson: Thank you, Dave!

www.ingramcontent.com/pod-product-compliance
Lightning Source LLC
Chambersburg PA
CBHW060025210326
41520CB00009B/1003